Contents

"What an absolutely brilliant resource! Team Ollerton have done the almost impossible, producing an accessible, engaging, faithful and deeply moving Bible overview for use in family worship. I anticipate *God's Story, Our Story* becoming a staple diet in our church's ministry to parents as they seek to share with the next generation the praiseworthy deeds of the Lord."

DAVE AND SALLY GOBBETT, Highfields Church, Cardiff and authors of *Hallelujah: Journeying Through Advent with Handel's Messiah*

"The Bible can feel overwhelming, especially for children, but *God's Story, Our Story* makes the big story clear and engaging for families. We've used an earlier version at home and can genuinely say it works—we loved walking through it together as a family and exploring what it means for our lives."

ANDY AND JO FROST, Share Jesus International and The Kitchen Table Project at Care for the Family

"A much-needed and long-awaited family resource. Andrew and Charlotte have carefully crafted this so that families can journey through the whole Bible together. It's in-depth but packaged in an accessible way—I can't wait to delve into this with my own family."

JOANNA ADEYINKA-BURFORD, TV Presenter on CBeebies, actor, and author of *What's Up*

"This is a rich and enduring resource for nurturing lifelong love for God's word in the home. The structure makes it natural for parents to read, discuss, pray and apply Scripture within the everyday rhythms of family life. At the same time, the book remains deeply rooted in the biblical text, inviting children not only to understand God's word but to recognize their place within his larger story. I am so excited to see the impact on families."

KAMI KINDEL, OneHope USA

"The whole Bible is for the whole family, and we've really appreciated the way *God's Story, Our Story* has helped us explore it together. It's accessible, engaging, interactive and doable. I love the simple rhythm of 'Hear it, read it, discuss it, pray it, do it, place it', which helps God's word move naturally into everyday life. I can't think of a more important activity to prioritise as we seek to follow Jesus together."

PAUL WOOLLEY, CEO of the London Institute of Contemporary Christianity (LICC)

"Join the Ollertons for a fun-filled, faith-fuelled adventure journey through the Bible for the whole family to enjoy! This resource is a brilliant biblical blend that will be a blessing to big kids and little kids alike. From the very beginning, you will be inspired again at how the Bible is one story that signposts us to the hero, Jesus himself. Whether used over coco pops, cooked dinners or a can of cola, this creative Ollerton collab will tantalise your truth tastebuds and satisfy the soul. We commend it to you!"

CATH AND DAI WOOLRIDGE, Chief Executive of Sound of Wales / Creative Specialist at Bible Society and award-winning poet

"What a brilliant resource! Accessible, inventive, biblical—a super-helpful guide to the Bible for people of all ages. Charlotte and Andrew have created a fabulous multimedia gift that retells, inspires and encourages. Children and adults will learn a lot and have fun as they do so, rediscovering the Good Book in a fresh and creative way. Hugely recommended! What a gem."

PAUL KERENSA, Comedian, broadcaster and author of the Fantastically Faithful series

"Fun, accessible and empowering for families!"

BEAR GRYLLS, Adventurer, TV Presenter, and Sunday Times bestselling author of *The Greatest Story Ever Told*

"Andrew and Charlotte are great guides for us to walk together through the whole glorious Bible story. God's big story is one that every family needs to hear—here's a nine-week adventure well worth going on!"

ED DREW, Ministry Director of Faith in Kids and author of *Raising Confident Kids*

"If your family is like most Christian families, you want to do a great job of spiritually leading your kids, but you are struggling with the how, the when and the what to do. *God's Story, Our Story* is a fantastic resource for any family. Whether you are brand new to reading the Bible as a family or you've been doing it regularly for years, this is a perfect answer for anyone asking how to orient their family around God."

ADAM GRIFFIN, Lead Pastor of Eastside Community Church in Dallas, Texas, and host of the Family Discipleship podcast

GOD'S STORY OUR STORY

a FAMILY JOURNEY through the BIBLE

thegoodbook COMPANY

CHARLOTTE & ANDREW OLLERTON

God's Story, Our Story

Published by:
The Good Book Company

thegoodbook.com | thegoodbook.co.uk
thegoodbook.com.au | thegoodbook.co.nz

Illustrated by Hsulynn Pang

Design by André Parker and Drew McCall

A CIP catalogue record for this book is available from the British Library.

ISBN: 9781802544404 | JOB-8600 | Printed in India

Week Eight: Easter

Week Nine: Mission

Before You Begin

Welcome to *God's Story, Our Story*—a bite-sized, multimedia journey through the Bible for the whole family. You'll travel from Genesis to Revelation in 45 sessions and discover how the Bible forms one great story. Meet the characters, explore the events and discover how you can be part of God's ongoing story and plan for our world!

This family resource is simple to run and fun to use. No prior knowledge is needed. We've written it to work for anyone who can sit still and chat for a while. (We think age 5 plus.)

Here's how it works...

The whole journey is made up of nine Bible story sets, with five sessions in each set. (So if you do this Monday to Friday, it will take nine weeks.) Four of the sessions are based on Bible stories and the fifth session is a memory verse that sums up the set. Each session should take a maximum of 15 minutes, and is probably do-able in 10.

Apart from memory-verse days, each session follows the same pattern:

Hear it: Each session begins with an overview of the Bible story for the day. You can either read the script yourselves or listen to us telling the story—follow the QR code to discover that option. For the first four sessions, there's also a video option you can QR-code your way to. Each story follows the same pattern: a scene-setting question connects to *Our Story*. Then we hear about a key Bible story and think about where it fits in *God's Story*. Finally, we reflect on what it means for our lives today.

Read it: There's a short Bible reading; we encourage you to find it and follow the passage in a print copy of the Bible.

Discuss it: Talk through the questions. (It's probably best if an adult leads this bit to keep the pace up.) Some questions are serious, some are a bit silly and others are more applied.

Pray it: Take a moment to be still and read the prayer.

Do it: This final suggestion gives a punchy and practical application.

We would also recommend you have a **Place it** moment at the end, using the *God's Story, Our Story Cards* that are designed to accompany this book. They can be found at thegoodbook.com/gods-story-cards. Each Bible story session has an accompanying card, with illustrations and key facts. As you do each session, hang, stick or prop each card up to form a visual Bible storyline in your own home. This installation will reinforce how the whole Bible fits together. (More information and game ideas are available with the card set.)

What's more, if your whole church would like to do *God's Story, Our Story* together, you'll find all-age talks for Sundays and some other church resources at thegoodbook.com/gods-story-resources. There you'll also find all the audio and video, and larger printouts of the images on the cards. Use the code printed at the bottom of this page to get access.

A final word from us, now that you're ready to go…

Over the last 18 years, we have loved gathering our three kids together over breakfast to read God's story, the Bible. It's never been dull! It's always been challenging, surprising and life-changing. Our prayer is that as you explore *God's Story, Our Story* together, it will shape and inspire your family story too. By the end, we hope you will see how the whole Bible fits together and feel better equipped to live your family story today.

Enjoy the journey!

Andrew and Charlotte

cfs5g4-a

Memory-Verse Days: Some Top Tips

It is a challenge to memorise God's words—and it is a gift. The Bible says that if we hide God's word in our hearts, we won't sin against him. His words also give us courage and comfort when things are tough.

For the fifth day in each set, as a family you can memorise a little part of the Bible. Each verse we've chosen summarises what you have looked at in your Bible stories that week. Each verse is printed in the book. If you have the *God's Story, Our Story Cards*, you'll find each verse on a card in that pack too—pop it into your Bible storyline once you have learned it.

There will be words to memorise and the location in the Bible where you can find them. For example, 1 Samuel chapter 16 verse 7 (Week 4's memory verse) will be written as 1 Samuel 16 v 7. It is from the story of David, when he is chosen to be king. It says, "People look at the outward appearance, but the LORD looks at the heart". (It's a great idea to go and find the verse in your Bible. You can find out where the book of the Bible is in the contents page.)

Here are some ideas of how you can memorise each verse. See what works the best for you. Don't be boring! You can have lots of fun trying to remember God's word.

Writing: Write the verse by hand on flash cards or post-it notes, or write the verse on a board. You could then do the "disappearing word game". Read it and then take away or rub out one word at a time, and then repeat, reciting it again and again after each word disappears. For example:

People ____________ at the outward appearance but the _________ looks at the ______________. 1 Samuel 16 v 7

Visualising: Create "word pictures" or use emojis to make the verse memorable. Draw these onto paper, replacing key words. For instance:

👱 👀 at the 👕 👖 but ✝️ 👀 at the ❤️

Actions: Decide on simple actions together to go with a key word from the verse.

People (point at various people in the room) look (pretend to hold binoculars to your eyes) at the outward appearance (grab your own top or t shirt and shake it about a bit), but the Lord (point up to the sky) looks (binoculars again) at the heart (do a heart shape with your fingers or hold your hand over the position where your heart is).

1 (hold up one finger) Samuel 16 (hold up one finger, then six fingers), verse 7 (hold up seven fingers).

Song: Turn the verse into a song by making up your own melody or using a well-known tune to sing your Bible-verse words to.

Audio recording: Record yourself reciting the passage and listen to it during daily activities such as driving or walking or brushing your teeth.

Digital apps: Try out apps like Remember Me or Anki. It's best to explore these beforehand to see how they work!

To really remember the verse well, simply repeat, repeat, repeat—in several different ways.

Week One

Beginnings

DAY 1

Creation: God Made It Good

GENESIS 1 – 2

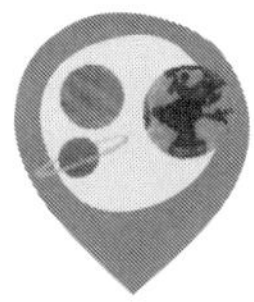

Our Story

The world is an amazing place, isn't it? The skies twinkle with lights. There are mountains to explore and oceans to swim in. Everywhere you look there is vibrant vegetation. The world is full of flying, leaping, running and buzzing things. It is all so good. On the very best of days it almost feels perfect!

God's Story

Our very first story from the Bible is about the beginning of everything and it starts very simply, with God. God wasn't lonely. But he did want to share his love and be in a relationship with people. He wanted to create a home for us to enjoy—and then create us to enjoy it.

Creation Story

In the very beginning it was dark. Silent. Still.

Imagine that! No light, no noise, no action.

But God was excited. He had so many ideas about what he wanted to do.

He knew we needed days and nights, darkness and light, waters and sky, land and seas. So, he spoke them into being with simple words, "Light!" "Sky!" "Land!" And there were islands, waterfalls and lakes.

These first three days of shaping and forming were good, but the land lacked colour and life. So God filled the world with grasses and bushes, fruits and flowers, vegetables and seeds. And trees. Many, many trees. Palm trees and pines, apple trees and alders, beech trees and baobab. God also made two extra-special trees—a tree of life and a tree of knowledge of good and evil.

Day four: the sky could be more fun... So, God filled it with stars, moons, planets and a big blazing sun.

Day five: the world was too silent... So, God filled it with many vibrant things. At his word the waters teemed with creatures: narwhal, sea cucumbers, orca and clown fish. And as he spoke the sky was flooded with flying features: ladybirds, hummingbirds, bald eagles and parrots.

Day six: it was time to create the animals—the weird and the wonderful, the ugly and the beautiful: sheep, chickens, wolves, zebras, iguanas, wombats and orangutans.

God again looked over all that he had made and declared it good. Good, but not very good.... Not perfect. Not full. Not complete. The world still lacked something, the best thing...

People!!! So God made them too. He moulded them out of the earth. He breathed his life into them. They were different to everything else God had made, because they were made to be like him. They talked and walked with him. They thought like him. God planted a garden for them to work in. And he told them to enjoy and look after everything he had made for them.

And finally, day seven: God stopped. God rested from all his work. God "Sabbathed". For everything was now very good. Everything was perfect.

God's Story

God put the first people in a garden called Eden, which means paradise. It was a safe place, a home where they could enjoy life with God. The Bible story starts in this perfect place, and despite everything that went wrong and that still goes wrong today, God promises that our story will one day finally return there.

Our Story

It is difficult for us to imagine a perfect world and perfect people. What must it have been like to be so close to God? Like you are walking and talking with him face to face? God made us to enjoy this special relationship with him, and we are going to see that through Jesus this is still possible.

Read It: Genesis 1 v 26-28, 31

> *Then God said, "Let us make mankind in our image, in our likeness, so that they may rule over the fish in the sea and the birds in the sky, over the livestock and all the wild animals, and over all the creatures that move along the ground."*

So God created mankind in his own image,
in the image of God he created them;
male and female he created them.

God blessed them and said to them, "Be fruitful and increase in number; fill the earth and subdue it. Rule over the fish in the sea and the birds in the sky and over every living creature that moves on the ground." …

God saw all that he had made, and it was very good. And there was evening, and there was morning—the sixth day.

Discuss It

- *What is your favourite thing that God created?*
- *What was God's favourite and best thing that he created?*
- *How does it make you feel to know that out of all the things God made, you are so special to God, and that he loves you and made this wonderful world for you?*
- *What do you think it means that God made us in his image to be like him?*

Pray It

Dear God, thank you for the amazing world you have made for us. Thank you that you made us to enjoy knowing you. Thank you that one day people will walk and talk with you in a perfect place again. Amen.

Do It

Keep your eyes peeled as you go about your day today—what could you say "wow" about, that God has made?

DAY 2

The Fall: Things Turn Bad

GENESIS 3

Our Story

Why are blackberries surrounded by thorns and often filled with worms? Why do our pets and family members get sick and sometimes die? Why is it easier to lie than to tell the truth and easier to be selfish than to be kind? It's not right. It's like something has broken and gone terribly wrong.

God's Story

Today's story takes us back to the moment when evil and sin entered the world. As we saw last time, God had not created things this way. In fact, Adam and Eve lived in a perfect world and could enjoy it for ever. The Garden of Eden was so perfect that only one rule was necessary; there was just one tree that was out of bounds. And this tree, the tree of the knowledge of good and evil, came with a warning: "When you eat from it you will certainly die." Can you imagine that? Only one rule! Easy enough, right?

The Fall Story

In the middle of the beautiful garden God had made stood a fruit tree. However, it was no ordinary fruit tree. Adam and Eve could work around it, sit under it, enjoy its shape and colour but God had clearly said they were not allowed to eat its fruit. They could eat from apple trees, pear trees, pomegranate trees and mango trees. They could pick and enjoy jack fruit and pomellos and plums but they could not eat fruit from this one tree. Because if they did they would die, God said. You see, this tree was different. It was a tree that gave knowledge about good and evil. And God didn't want Adam and Eve to understand or experience evil...

One day a crafty snake strikes up a conversation with Eve. He plays with her mind. He sows doubts in her soul. Maybe the forbidden fruit is what she needs to be happy and successful? Maybe eating it will make her like God knowing and deciding what is good and what is evil? Eve listens. She decides not to trust God. She eats and passes the fruit to Adam—who also ignores God's loving warning. They both disobey God—they both sin.

One rule is broken, two choices are made and things begin to go terribly wrong.

They feel embarrassed.

They feel afraid.

They run from God

They hide.

They lie.

They snitch.

They blame each other.

And death and evil enter the world.

Because Adam and Eve had eaten the fruit and disobeyed God, their relationship with each other was broken. They were disconnected from God. God still loved them but life would now be tough and painful, and life would now end. God said they must leave his presence and the garden.

God's Story

Yet, as God turned Adam and Eve away from the garden he began a great rescue plan. He clothed them with animal skins. That's right, an animal was sacrificed to cover for Adam and Eve. Hold that thought because this points to another sacrifice years later that would heal hurt, destroy death, mend relationships and bring people back to God.

God also gave the first people a promise. He promised that one day another person would come who would always choose right and crush that crafty snake once and for all. One day, there would be no more death, loneliness or fear.

Our Story

The sacrifice and the promise as Adam and Eve leave Eden of course both point to Jesus. He is the snake crusher that appears throughout the Bible story to put everything right again. He came so that you, and anyone who trusts in him, can look forward to being in a new, perfect creation with God, a place like Eden, where we will no longer experience death or loneliness or fear.

Read It: Genesis 3 v 1-6, 21, 23

Now the snake was more crafty than any of the wild animals the LORD God had made. He said to the woman, "Did God really say, 'You must not eat from any tree in the garden'?"

The woman said to the snake, "We may eat fruit from the trees in the garden, but God did say, 'You must not eat fruit from the tree that is in the middle of the garden, and you must not touch it, or you will die.'"

"You will not certainly die," the snake said to the woman. "For God knows that when you eat from it your eyes will be opened, and you will be like God, knowing good and evil."

When the woman saw that the fruit of the tree was good for food and pleasing to the eye, and also desirable for gaining wisdom, she took some and ate it. She also gave some to her husband, who was with her, and he ate it ...

The LORD God made garments of skin for Adam and his wife and clothed them ... the LORD God banished him from the Garden of Eden to work the ground from which he had been taken.

Discuss It

- *Why is it good to have rules? What rules do you have to follow?*
- *What one rule did God give Adam and Eve, and why?*
- *What sad changes happened when Adam and Eve disobeyed God?*
- *Why is life so much better if we do what God tells us?*
- *How has this story made you more grateful for what Jesus came to do?*

Pray It

Dear God, thank you that you care for us and know what is best for us. Thank you that you love us even when we disobey you. Please help us to do what you ask and not give in to temptation. Thank you for sending Jesus as a sacrifice to sort out our sin. Amen.

Do It

When making choices today, think, "What would God want me to do?"

And don't talk to snakes!

DAY 3

The Flood: World Washed Clean

GENESIS 6 – 9

Our Story

Have you ever played spot the odd one out where one thing is clearly different to the others? Say, a ballet shoe amongst football boots?

Have you ever experienced feeling like the odd one out? Maybe because you didn't make the school team or you don't have the coolest shoes?

Or, maybe because you believe something different to those around you?

God's Story

Today's story is about someone who was the odd one out. It begins a long time after the world was made. God is sad because the world is no longer "very good" or even "good". It's violent and wicked. Everyone is only evil all the time. Imagine that! And this filled God's heart with pain, so much so that God decided to start all over again.

The Flood Story

As God looked to see who to use to be part of his rescue plan there was only one clear option. This man was different. He was the odd one out. He was blameless among the people of his time, and he walked with God. He was not corrupt or wicked or violent. He did everything God asked him to do. So when God told him to build a massive boat, even though he lived nowhere near the sea, he did. Which made him odder still…

"Right then," said Noah, "All done. Now that we've finished the water-proofing, the animals will come."

The neighbours had already arrived. They'd set up their chairs. They were watching, pointing and laughing.

"Building a boat!" one giggled.

"'The animals will come'" another smirked.

"Noah says it's going to rain for 40 days and nights!" another roared with laughter, slapping his thigh.

"Everything will be destroyed, he says... ha ha ha."

"What a joke."

"What a foolish, odd, old man!"

Then two by two the animals began to arrive—slithering snakes, galloping giraffes, hopping hares, bounding baboons, climbing koalas, leaping leopards and flapping finches. Two by two they continued to come, until all kinds of creatures were on board.

"Welcome, welcome. In y'all go," Noah shouted. "We'll get you some food. You can soon have a snooze. The floodgates of heaven are about to open."

"In you all go too!" Noah said to his family. "God will close the door. He'll save us and protect us."

And then it began to rain. For 40 days the rain kept coming. Waters gurgled up from the deep and rain lashed down from above. Puddles turned to streams and then to rivers and then to seas. Everything was covered. The world was having a wash.

And then the rain stopped. And for the next eleven months the waters receded. Seas returned to being rivers. Streams became puddles again. And then God told Noah to leave the ark.

"God has saved us and protected us!" Noah shouted joyfully to his family and the animals. "Out you all go!"

And the animals and people poured out—cheering, woofing, braying and chirping with delight. This was a fresh start, and God told Noah's family to go out and enjoy it.

God's Story

This was a second chance for the world but God knew that people would still not trust and obey him. So he strung a beautiful bow across the sky as a promise that there would never be another flood. But this rainbow also pointed to his promise of a person who would bring a rescue plan that would be for all people and last for all time.

Our Story

Noah was so different. What a role model! He walked closely with God when everyone else was ignoring him. He did what God asked even when it seemed totally crazy. He was the odd one out. Be courageous if you feel like the odd one out sometimes and if people laugh at you for your faith in God. God is looking for people like Noah who are different and who will be part of his plan of salvation.

Read It: Genesis 6 v 9-15

This is the account of Noah and his family.

Noah was a righteous man, blameless among the people of his time, and he walked faithfully with God. Noah had three sons: Shem, Ham and Japheth.

Now the earth was corrupt in God's sight and was full of violence. God saw how corrupt the earth had become, for all the people on earth had corrupted their ways. So God said to Noah, "I am going to put an end to all people, for the earth is filled with violence because of them. I am surely going to destroy both them and the earth. So make yourself an ark of cypress wood; make rooms in it and coat it with pitch inside and out.

Discuss It

- *If you were stuck on the ark, which animal would you want to share a bedroom with and why?*
- *Why did God flood the earth?*
- *What was different about Noah—why was he the odd one out?*
- *Have you ever felt different or weird because you follow God?*
- *How has Noah's bravery and determination to be different by following God challenged or encouraged you?*

Pray It

Dear God, thank you for saving Noah's family when you washed the world clean. Help us to live as your friends and do what you ask us to do, even if that means being different. Amen.

Do It

Draw a rainbow. Keep it with you. Remember that God keeps his promises and he cares for you.

DAY 4

The Tower: The People Scatter

GENESIS 11:1-9

Our Story

Have you got any top skills or special talents? Maybe you can do a record-breaking number of cartwheels, grow prize-winning carrots or name all the capital cities of the world? What would it be like if everyone knew your name because you had done something amazing or had an incredible talent?

But what if there's something way more important than just trying to make a name for yourself?

God's Story

There is a big jump in time between Noah and the flood and today's story about the tower of Babel. There are now many families living and working together in a place called Shinar, a flat fertile area in modern Iraq. But just like in Noah's day, they have totally forgotten about God. They are thinking only about themselves, their skills and talents and how great they could be... It all looks very impressive and under their control.

The Tower Story

The people had built a big, bold, beautiful city. It was magnificent. It was their pride and joy. However, now they wanted to do more, something that would amaze and excite. This creation would be even bigger, bolder and more beautiful. It would reflect their brilliance and brains. It would get the whole world talking about them...

The people on Shinar plain got together. They talked, discussed, negotiated and decided. They were so proud of themselves, their plans, tools, technology and talents.

They would construct a tower, a ziggurat, like in the surrounding cities. However, their tower would be taller and stronger; their tower would reach the heavens. Their tower would not only have stairs and a temple on top—it would be a stairway to heaven! Their tower would be famous. *They* would be famous—more famous than God!

Architects articulated the plan.

Engineers talked through the technical challenges.

Craftsmen chatted as they made bricks from mud.

Builders bantered and bellowed instructions.

Manual labourers mumbled.

Babies babbled and children cheered.

Nothing and no one could stop them!

And all this time God was watching with amusement and concern. He was amused that they thought they could actually reach heaven and he was concerned that they wanted to build a world without him. "No, this can't continue," he decided. "I'll have to stop them. They are far too full of themselves, too powerful. Together like this they will do more harm than good. Let's go down to them and confuse their languages, so they cannot understand each other."

So God did. He confused their languages. And a cacophony of nonsense filled the air. Nothing made sense. The people could no longer talk, discuss, negotiate and decide together. The building work ground to a halt.

And with no language to unite them, they separated and spread out over the world. Far from making a great name for themselves, these proud people, in their confusion, could only babble.

God's Story

The people in Shinar had totally forgotten about their great God. They were thinking only about themselves and how great they could be. God needed to remind them that he is the greatest and that they would be far more fulfilled by knowing him and being part of his story, rather than ignoring him and trying to write their own. So rather than becoming famous for their building project, they became infamous for ignoring God.

Our Story

God has given all of us special skills and talents. But we need to be careful, because when we are good at something or successful in something it can make us feel important, safe and secure. We can begin to ignore God. It's always best to make sure people hear about how great God is, not how amazing we are.

Read It: Genesis 11 v 1, 4-9

Now the whole world had one language and a common speech …

Then they said, "Come, let us build ourselves a city, with a tower that reaches to the heavens, so that we may make a name for ourselves; otherwise we will be scattered over the face of the whole earth."

But the LORD came down to see the city and the tower the people were building. The LORD said, "If as one people speaking the same language they have begun to do this, then nothing they plan to do will be impossible for them. Come, let us go down and confuse their language so they will not understand each other."

So the LORD scattered them from there over all the earth, and they stopped building the city. That is why it was called Babel—because there the LORD confused the language of the whole world. From there the LORD scattered them over the face of the whole earth.

Discuss It

- *Why did the people try to build a big city and great tower?*
- *In what ways do people show off and try to become famous today?*
- *Be honest—how are you tempted to show off and try to make a name for yourself?*
- *How can we make sure we are a team with God in what we say, do and think today?*

Pray It

Dear God, help us to always remember your greatness. Help us not to become proud, or too successful, so that we forget about you. In everything we do, help us to make your name great. Amen.

Do It

Find out how to say "Hello" and "Thank you" in another language that you don't already know.

DAY 5

Memory Verse

"In the beginning God created the heavens and the earth."

GENESIS 1 v 1

VERSE-MEMORISING TOP TIPS

Write It
Visualise It
Act It
Sing It
Record It
Use an App
... and repeat, repeat, repeat!

Week Two

Families

DAY 6

Abraham: God Makes a Promise

GENESIS 12 – 21

Our Story

Have you made any promises this week? Sometimes we promise not to tell, or to be someone's best friend or to try harder. Sometimes the promises people make are totally crazy. Deep down they know they can't keep them. But can you imagine someone making an impossible promise that they are actually able to keep?

God's Story

Our Bible story today is about a series of seemingly crazy promises that God made, and kept. It is about 2,000 years before Jesus lived on earth. Again, people are ignoring God. But in today's story God's salvation plan takes a new turn. It's time to begin building a nation of people that God can call his own. His attention turns to one particular flourishing, moon-god-worshipping city, Haran, where his eyes lock onto a 75-year-old childless man and his wife...

Abraham's Story

The first time God visited Abraham and Sarah he gave them three laugh-out-loud, crazy, almost unbelievable, outrageously wonderful promises... He promised they would become a great people, they would live in a great land and they would be a great blessing to everyone!

Abraham and Sarah were old and childless, but they responded obediently when God asked them to move from the comfort of Haran to a strange new land. God showed them the way, and when they arrived he visited and reminded them of the wonderful things to come. And God added another promise; this land of

Canaan would one day belong to their family.

"This is crazy," Abraham thought.

"Unbelievable," Sarah whispered.

During the third visit Abraham questioned God. "You have promised me a family," Abraham said, "but you have given me no children".

God took him outside. "Look up at the sky and count the stars. Your family will be more numerous than those."

On his fourth visit , God's promise was even more amazing: "Sarah will give you a son and kings will come from your family." And what do you think Abraham did when he heard this? He fell face down before God and laughed. "Will a son really be born to me? I'm 100 years old, and Sarah is 90..."

By now Abraham and Sarah had waited on God's laugh-out-loud, almost unbelievable, outrageously wonderful promises for 24 years. They were ancient. A baby, nations and kings coming from *them*? At their age? This was impossible!

On visit number five the Lord brought friends. Sarah made dinner. They talked. "This time next year your wife will have a son," they said.

Now it was Sarah's turn. She grinned, smirked and chuckled to herself in disbelief. And the Lord asked, "Why is Sarah laughing? Is anything too hard for God?"

Sure enough, one year later, as promised, Abraham and Sarah had a son. And guess what they called him? Isaac, meaning "he laughs".

The laugh-out-loud, crazy, almost unbelievable, outrageously wonderful promises Abraham and Sarah had been given had started to come true. Do you see? Nothing is too hard for God.

God's Story

Abraham and Sarah learned to trust God, and their family grew into a nation that God called his own, more numerous than the stars in the sky or the sand on the shores—just as God had promised.

Two thousand years after Isaac, from Abraham's family came another miracle child whose birth didn't just seem impossible, it *was* impossible. He would fulfil all the great promises God made to Abraham. Through him blessing and friendship with God is offered to all families—including yours. Can you guess his name?

Our Story

God always keeps his promises. Always. God's made so many promises throughout the Bible that we can't take a step forward without treading on one.

Remember, nothing is impossible with God and in Jesus, all God's promises are good to go. He promises forgiveness, peace, his presence with us wherever we go. He promises a forever home with him in heaven if we are his friends.

Read It: Genesis 12 v 1-3

The LORD had said to Abram, "Go from your country, your people and your father's household to the land I will show you.

"I will make you into a great nation,
and I will bless you;
I will make your name great,
and you will be a blessing.
I will bless those who bless you,
and whoever curses you I will curse;
and all peoples on earth
will be blessed through you."

Discuss It

- *Which do you think there are more of—grains of sand on the beaches or stars in the universe?*
  (Answer: Scientists estimate that there are even more stars than sand. Wow!)
- *How does the birth of Isaac start to fulfil the massive promises God made to Abraham?*
- *Which of God's promises to us are you most excited about?*
- *Have you or your family ever had to wait for God to fulfil one of his promises to you?*
- *What promises are you still waiting for him to keep?*

Pray It

Dear God, you made more stars in the sky than there are grains of sand on the beaches. Yet you know and love me. Thank you for the promises you have made to me and the laughter you have in store for me. Help me to trust you and to wait patiently for you to keep all your amazing promises. Amen.

Do It

On a clear night do some stargazing or the next time you are at the beach see how you get on with counting the grains of sand there. Thank God for keeping his promises.

DAY 7

Isaac: Trust God

GENESIS 22

Our Story

How often do you travel in a car? You probably do not take a lot of time thinking about whether you trust your car before you get in it. You have ridden in it many times before and been safe. It's reliable. You trust it. Hopefully, you feel the same about the person who drives you! From experience over time you know that they love you and that you can trust them.

God's Story

In today's story, Abraham will have to lean all his weight on God and trust him through the toughest test. Isaac, the promised miracle child who was Sarah and Abraham's only son and the first child in the enormous nation God promised to build, is now older. Remember his name means "He laughs"? Be warned, today's story does not contain much laughter. However, it's crammed full of questions and an amazing example of trust.

Isaac's Story

Isaac was full of questions...

Dad, why has God asked us to go on a three-day adventure?

Where is Mount Moriah anyway? It sounds creepy!

Why do we need to go so far away for the sacrifice?

Do you think I will make it to the top?

Isaac's curiosity usually made Abraham laugh. But not today. Not on this journey.

Why can't Mum come? I'd rather she came than the servants.

Why are you cutting and loading so much wood onto the donkey? Can't we find it on the way?

On the third day, even more questions spilled out.

Why are you promising the servants that we will both return? Why wouldn't we both come back?

Are you making me carry the wood for the offering because I am stronger than the donkey?

As the going got steeper, the questions got even trickier...

Dad, I see you have a knife and burning coals—but where is the lamb for the sacrifice?

Dad, Dad, what is the most difficult thing God has ever asked you to do?

How could Abraham explain that *this* was the most difficult thing God had ever asked him to do, because somehow God wanted Isaac to be the sacrifice? He took a deep breath. "Child, God himself will provide the lamb for the offering."

They walked on. Abraham trusted God totally but he also had questions. Without Isaac how would God build a family, a nation, a salvation plan? How would God keep his promises? And, could he go through with this?

At the top of the mountain Abraham arranged the wood. He tied Isaac up. He laid Isaac down. He took the knife. He raised his hand...

"Abraham!" a voice called from heaven. "Stop! See that sheep trapped in that bush? Take it and sacrifice it instead of your son."

"See", Abraham said to Isaac: "I knew we could trust God to provide a lamb for the offering. We will both return—like I said we would."

Isaac probably asked many more questions on the way down.

Dad, have you heard a voice from heaven before?

Do you think you are the oldest person to ever climb Mount Moriah?

And the reply? Well, most probably, Abraham laughed!

God's Story

Abraham knew God loved him because God had cared for him and kept his promises for years. So, even when it was difficult and didn't make sense, Abraham trusted and obeyed God completely.

Did you know that Mount Moriah is near where the city of Jerusalem was later built? So the hill that Abraham's son Isaac climbed carrying the wood, God's Son Jesus then climbed, carrying a wooden cross. However, there was no voice from heaven for Jesus, no lamb to swap in for him. He *did* die. He *was* the sacrifice—the sacrifice that God provided so that we could be saved.

Our Story

Think about how you trust the person who drives your car. God is even more reliable. If God was willing to give his only Son, Jesus, and if Jesus was prepared to die for us as our sacrifice, we can trust God with everything. Later on in the Bible, in a book called Proverbs, it says, "Trust in the LORD with all your heart and lean not on your own understanding" (Proverbs 3 v 5). Like Abraham, we can trust God with everything we have and in everything we do.

Read It: Genesis 22 v 13-14

> *Abraham looked up and there in a thicket he saw a ram caught by its horns. He went over and took the ram and sacrificed it as a burnt offering instead of his son. So Abraham called that place The LORD Will Provide. And to this day it is said, "On the mountain of the LORD it will be provided".*

Discuss It

- *Which people do you most trust, and why?*
- *How was Abraham able to trust God when God asked him to do this very difficult thing?*
- *Can you think about any similarities and differences between this story and God giving his Son, Jesus, to die for us?*
- *How does knowing we can trust God totally mean we can obey him when it's difficult?*
- *How is God asking you to do this at the moment?*

Pray It

Dear God, Abraham trusted and obeyed you because you proved that you loved him and kept your promises to him. Thank you for loving us and sending Jesus to die for us. Thank you for keeping your promises. Help us to trust and obey you too. Amen.

Do It

Play a trust game. Ask an adult that you trust to stand behind you. Ask them to catch you when you fall backwards. Close your eyes and fall back into their arms. Now switch places, and you catch the adult!

DAY 8

Jacob: God Gives a Name

GENESIS 25 – 33

Our Story

Names are very important. In our family, we chose three amazing names: Lucy means "bringer of light"; Joel means "the Lord is God"; and Toby means "God is good". Do you have any idea what your name means? Do you know the reason you were given your name? Maybe you could ask the person who gave it to you…

God's Story

Abraham's name means "father of nations". His son's name, Isaac, means "laughter". In today's story, Isaac has grown up. He has twin boys of his own. Their names tell us about them. As we'll see, God does not choose perfect people, and life with God is not always easy. God does not always do the obvious or normal thing to carry out his rescue plan.

Jacob's Story

As they grew inside Rebekah, Isaac's wife, the twins wrestled, jostled and shoved. Esau came out first. "We'll name him 'Esau'," said Isaac, "because he is red". The second twin came out grabbing Esau's ankle. "Let's call him Jacob, the 'heel grabber'," said Isaac. "He will be a tricky one."

As the boys grew, Rebekah plotted to make Jacob the leader and heir. (At this time the oldest boy was normally the boss and inherited everything—including, in the case of this special family, God's promises and blessing.)

"Jacob," Rebekah whispered one day, "your father is old and blind. Quick, disguise yourself to look and smell like your wild, red, hairy twin. Take him dinner. Grab God's blessing from your father before your brother returns."

"JACOB!!!" Esau the wild, the hairy, the red, yelled when he found out. "I'LL HUNT YOU DOWN. I'LL SMASH YOU AND BASH YOU FOR STEALING MY BLESSING."

But no one replied, because Jacob the trickster had fled...

Exhausted from running, Jacob slept. He dreamt that angels were going up and down a staircase between heaven and earth and God spoke to him: "All people on earth will be blessed through you".

Hopeful now, Jacob continued on to his uncle Laban's house. Here, although he was mistreated and tricked Jacob grew rich, married twice and had twelve sons. However, after 20 years he longed to go home and put things right.

While he was alone on the last evening of the return journey, a mysterious stranger visited Jacob. They wrestled, jostled and shoved. Jacob was used to getting what he wanted, but he could not win and the stranger could not lose—with one flick he dislocated Jacob's hip.

Suddenly Jacob knew that he was wrestling with God. He clung to him—for God alone could give him the blessing and love he had struggled for all his life. "Jacob," the stranger said, "your new name is 'Israel', which means 'you have wrestled with God'".

Jacob knew he was now ready to meet Esau.

"JACOB!!!" Esau yelled. He was still red, wild and hairy—but he no longer wanted to smash or bash his twin. Esau grabbed his brother, but they didn't wrestle, jostle or shove. They had a huge hairy hug.

"I'm not Jacob," Jacob said, "Call me Israel, for I've wrestled with God. I've changed."

God's Story

Jacob was the youngest son and he was a cheat. However, he was God's unlikely choice to see his promise to bless the whole world move forward. Jacob got so many things wrong. But God still used him and changed him from being a trickster full of fear to being a man who knew he needed God and who wanted to be part of God's plan.

Our Story

Whatever your name is and whatever it means, you can be part of God's wonderful plan. You may feel you have failed like Jacob, but God has not written you off. Remember, God does not choose perfect people. No matter what you have done God can still use you because he can bless you and change you.

Read It: Genesis 32 v 24-28, 30

Jacob was left alone, and a man wrestled with him till daybreak. When the man saw that he could not overpower him, he touched the socket of Jacob's hip so that his hip was wrenched as he wrestled with the man. Then the man said, "Let me go, for it is daybreak."

But Jacob replied, "I will not let you go unless you bless me."

The man asked him, "What is your name?"

"Jacob," he answered.

Then the man said, "Your name will no longer be Jacob, but Israel, because you have struggled with God and with humans and have overcome." ...

So Jacob called the place Peniel, saying, "It is because I saw God face to face, and yet my life was spared."

Discuss It

- *Why was Jacob not a very obvious choice to be the person to carry forward God's salvation plan?*
- *When Jacob clung to the mysterious heavenly stranger, what did he realise he most needed?*
- *Jacob limped off the next day knowing God would be with him. How do you think this changed the way he felt about meeting Esau?*
- *How does knowing that God is with you help you with any challenges you are facing?*

Pray It

Close your eyes and think about a challenge you are facing. We are now going to bring it to God in prayer.

Dear Father, you know the situation I am thinking about and my fears. Come and be with me. Remind me that the thing I most need is your blessing. Help me to have confidence to take on every challenge. Amen.

Do It

Next time you feel afraid of a situation, tell yourself, "God is with me and he loves me. We can do this!"

DAY 9

Joseph: God Works It Out

GENESIS 37 – 50

Our Story

In the last few months what has been a high point for you? Maybe you won a competition, went somewhere special or mastered a skill? Maybe you have had some tricky times too, some low points? Maybe people have been mean to you? Or things have not gone according to plan? Maybe you got blamed for something you didn't do?

God's Story

Today's story is about Jacob (renamed Israel), his family and especially his second-youngest son, Joseph. Joseph's life had many highs and lows. It's just like a rollercoaster ride—and, through all the ups and downs, God is amazingly at work.

Joseph's Story

"Snitch!"

"I hate him."

"I hate him *more*."

Joseph's ten older brothers were complaining bitterly—again.

"Why do we have to do the dirty, hard, sheep work?"

"While he lazes around at home with Dad, in that *coat*."

"I hate his special, colourful coat."

"I hate his boasting and dreams."

"Come, let's kill him..."

So they threw young Joseph down a well.
And left him there, for dead.
But realising they could make some cash
They sold him as a slave instead.

Transported to Egypt.
Bought by Potiphar (the captain of Pharaoh's guard),
Forced into work...
How low could Joe go?

The household was large.
Joe worked hard.
He was put in charge.
Things looked up.
Joe was on top.

But then he was falsely accused.
Innocent, with spirit bruised
Down to prison he went, confused.

But God was with him; he showed Joseph kindness and gave him success in everything.

The king's prison was large.
Joe again worked hard.
Was put in charge.
Things looked up.
Joe was on top.

The King's baker and cupbearer were also in prison.
Joe explained their dreams with amazing wisdom.
When the cupbearer was freed,
He promised Joe release.

Some two years passed.
Time was slow.
This was a new low.
The cupbearer forgot. But God had not.

Then Pharaoh had some very strange dreams
That no one in court understood.
Then the cupbearer remembered that Joe was in jail
And thought, "He can help, I know Joe won't fail".

When Joseph was told of Pharaoh's visions

He interpreted them with amazing precision.

Up Joseph went in the King's estimation.
Up in responsibility.
Up to the position of prime minister of Egypt.
He married.
Had two children...
Up and up and up.

Seven years of up.
Seven years of storing up grain.

Then a massive international down—
Drought and famine all around.
Hunger for everyone, including Joe's brothers,
who came down to Egypt to restock their cupboards.

Joseph didn't hate them—not one little bit.
He'd forgiven and forgotten his time in the pit .

He explained how their harm
God had turned into good.
How his lows became highs
And he now understood
God's purpose through it all to bring his salvation
To his life, and their lives, and the whole of the nation.

Such highs.
Such lows.
Go God!
Go Joe!

God's Story

What a rollercoaster! Interestingly, God seemed closest to Joseph in his lowest times—times which he used to change Joseph. When he met his brothers who had been so horrible to him, he didn't punish them but forgave them. Joseph's food plan saved his family from starvation in the famine. He became a person in a powerful position who God could use for "the saving of many lives". One day his future family member, Jesus, would save the world not from starvation but from sin. He would go down to the ultimate low of death so we could rise up to life with God.

Our Story

How are things at the moment? Remember, when life is tough and tricky God is right there with you. So trust him. He will work things out for your good. It's helpful to remember like Joseph did that God is with you and he can sort things that seem impossible for you.

Read It: Genesis 45 v 4, 5, 7; 50 v 19-20

Then Joseph said to his brothers … "I am your brother Joseph, the one you sold into Egypt! And now, do not be distressed and do not be angry with yourselves for selling me here, because it was to save lives that God sent me ahead of you … But God sent me ahead of you to preserve for you a remnant on earth and to save your lives by a great deliverance" …

[Another time] Joseph said to them, "Don't be afraid. Am I in the place of God? You intended to harm me, but God intended it for good to accomplish what is now being done, the saving of many lives."

Discuss It

- *How many of the tough things that happened to Joseph can you remember?*
- *How did God change Joseph through the low times?*
- *How was God's plan to save many lives worked out through Joseph?*
- *How is God's greater plan of salvation worked out through Jesus?*
- *When we face tough and tricky times, what can we learn from Joseph's story?*

Pray It

Thank you, God, that you have a good plan for my life, even when tough stuff happens. Thank you for being with me in the highs and lows. Thank you that your good plans are being worked out even when I can't see it. I trust you to work it all out. Amen.

Do It

At the end of today think back—what has been a high point and a low point? Stretch up high and tell God about the best thing. Crouch down low and tell him about the toughest thing. Remember, he is with you all the time, even when things are tricky!

DAY 10

Memory Verse

"I will bless those who bless you... and all peoples on earth will be blessed through you."

GENESIS 12 v 3

VERSE-MEMORISING TOP TIPS

Write It

Visualise It

Act It

Sing It

Record It

Use an App

... and repeat, repeat, repeat!

Week Three

Journey

DAY 11

Moses: The Rescue Plan

EXODUS 1 – 4

Our Story

Have you ever been given a task to do and you felt that you just could not do it? Or been given a challenge and you could not see a way to start it, let alone see it through? Maybe it was an important role in a performance or a tricky school project? Maybe it made you want to shout, "I'm not good enough!" or "I can't do this!"

God's Story

It's almost 300 years after Joseph. His family, the Israelites, have become a great people, living in Egypt. But Egypt is no longer safe. Pharaoh, the ruler, is scared the Israelites will rise up and fight him so he has enslaved them and started killing them. They are labouring hard on Pharaoh's big building projects and losing hope. In today's story we read about how God had not forgotten his people nor his promises. During the great famine, God had kept Abraham's descendants alive. But how will he rescue his people from slavery now?

Moses' Story

God's rescue plan began with five women.

Two brave midwives refused Pharaoh's order to kill newborn Israelite boys. A mother and daughter courageously smuggled a baby into a basket and floated him down the River Nile, right into the care of woman number five, Pharaoh's own daughter. She named him Moses and took him into the palace where he, an Israelite, was educated as a leader right under Pharaoh's nose!

However, Moses never quite fitted in. How could he when his people were so cruelly treated? One day, saddened and enraged, he killed an Egyptian and ran far away to Midian, where he looked after sheep.

A long time passed, until one normal shepherding day at Mount Sinai Moses saw a bush alight—but not burning up—and it was talking! Moses soon realised it was not the bush speaking; it was God. And he had some massive announcements to make…

This is a holy place. Moses, you must take off your sandals. (Which he did).

I have seen my people suffering, and I am going to rescue them and bring them into an amazing new land.

I am sending you to be their leader.

Moses, you must go now.

However, Moses did not want to go now.

He had a few things to say in reply…

One: Who am I to do this task?

Two: What shall I tell the people your name is?

Three: What if people don't listen or believe me?

Four: I don't do public speaking!

Five: Send someone else!

For each question, God had an answer—and for each excuse, a response…

One: I will be with you.

Two: Tell the people my name is I AM WHO I AM.

Three: I'll enable you to do amazing signs so people will listen—your shepherd's staff will become a snake, your leprous hand will be healed.

Four: I will tell you what to say and your brother Aaron will help you.

Five: I've chosen you. Now go!

So Moses and his family returned to Egypt. He and Aaron told the Israelite slaves about God's plans. They performed the signs. And they worshipped God together.

God's Story

God heard his people's cries. He saw their pain. And because of his love and promises, he planned a way out of their misery and slavery. God said to Moses, "I have come down to rescue them".

Centuries later, this is what Jesus did. He came from heaven to earth to set us free from our misery and pain. He did this by saving us from our sin, which lies under all the harm we do to each other. Jesus is God's way out for all people, not just the Israelites.

Our Story

Maybe you know someone who is in a difficult situation, is sad or is feeling trapped. They need your help and they need to hear about Jesus. Will you be like Moses, who wanted God to send someone else to help? Will you say, "I can't do this"? Or will you be brave, knowing that God is with you, and will you do something to help?

Read It: Exodus 3 v 7, 10-12

> *The Lord said [to Moses], "I have indeed seen the misery of my people in Egypt. I have heard them crying out because of their slave drivers, and I am concerned about their suffering ... So now, go. I am sending you to Pharaoh to bring my people the Israelites out of Egypt."*
>
> *But Moses said to God, "Who am I that I should go to Pharaoh and bring the Israelites out of Egypt?"*
>
> *And God said, "I will be with you..."*

Discuss It

- *What would you do if a burning bush called your name?!*
- *What was God's task for Moses?*
- *How did Moses feel about being sent back to Egypt on a rescue mission?*
- *What did God promise him?*
- *It might be the first time you've thought about this, but what might God's mission be for you and your family? He's with you whatever it is.*

Pray It

Dear God, sometimes I feel like I am not able to do what you ask me to do. Thank you that you are powerful and promise to be with me. Help me not to run away but to take care of those in need and tell them about you. Amen.

Do It

Find out about what God's people are doing to help those who are still in slavery today: https://www.modernslaveryeducation.com/slaverytoday

DAY 12

Passover: The Blood of the Lamb

EXODUS 6 – 12

Our Story

Which would you choose if you had to endure one of the following?

- Sleep the night in a bed of frogs
- Play a sports match in total darkness
- Go to school covered in boils and sores
- Swim a length of a swimming pool full of blood

Surely if you faced one of these horrible things, you'd do anything to make it stop. Wouldn't you?

God's Story

God promised Moses that he would rescue his people from Egypt. But there's no way Pharaoh is going to let his free workforce leave, is there? In today's story we will see that this is not just a battle over slaves. It is also a battle of might and truth. We will find out who is the most powerful. Will it be Israel's God or the gods Pharaoh believes in—like Rah, the sun god or Sobek, the crocodile god who controlled the River Nile?

Passover Story

Moses stood before Pharaoh, trembling, and gave him God's message. But Pharaoh was having none of it.

"A god called 'I AM WHO I AM'? Never heard of him! Let these people go so they can worship God in the desert? No, nope, never!" he said.

Even when Moses performed incredible signs, Pharaoh was not impressed. "So what if you can throw your staff on the ground and it turns into a cobra. My magicians can do that too—go on!

"Oh—your cobra ate my cobras...

"But it's still NO!"

Moses met Pharaoh on his morning stroll by the Nile. "I AM WHO I AM says, 'Let my people go, so they may worship me,'" Moses said.

"No, nope, never!"

"Well then, blood will fill the Nile, your buckets and jars." And it did.

Moses visited the palace again. "God's sending a frog plague. Frogs in your beds, bowls and chariots. Let God's people go!"

"No, nope, never!" said Pharaoh.

"Anyway, my magicians can do blood and frog tricks too!"

After the plague of gnats, God protected his people, but hardships for Egypt continued. Dense swarms of flies filled houses and ruined their land. Cattle died. Festering boils covered people and animals. Huge hailstones beat down. Locusts devoured everything. A darkness so menacing that it could be felt lasted for three days.

Each time, Moses said "I AM WHO I AM says 'Let my people go'". Each time, Pharaoh responded, "No, nope, never!" And the more Pharaoh refused, the worse the plagues became.

When Moses went to the palace for a tenth time, he issued a final warning from God: the oldest boy in every household would die that night if Pharaoh did not let the Israelites go. But Pharaoh remained hard-hearted and stubborn: "NO, NOPE, NEVER!"

"Families, paint a lamb's blood around your doors," said Moses. "This is the final and most deadly plague. Stay inside. When he sees the lamb's blood, God will pass over your house and protect you. Roast the lamb. Eat with sandals on and bags packed. For tomorrow there will be the loudest wailing throughout Egypt that there ever will be. But we will be free."

That night Moses was summoned. "Up! Leave!" cried the distraught Pharaoh. "GO! Go worship the Lord as you have requested."

God's Story

Because God loved his people, he gave them special instructions so that death would pass over their homes and they would be saved. This may sound a bit strange (especially if you like lambs more than your older brother!) but the lambs' blood points forward to someone else. He died during Passover, the festival celebrating God's rescue of the people from Egypt. Jesus said his blood was going to rescue people too. One of his many names is the Lamb of God.

Our Story

The Passover story is about escaping death and being set free. To experience this, the Israelites had to trust in God's salvation plan. They had to act in faith by painting blood onto the door posts. In the same way, we have to act in faith by believing that Jesus died for us so that we, all these years later, can escape God's judgment and be set free from sin.

Read It: Exodus 12 v 21-23

> *Moses summoned all the elders of Israel and said to them, "Go at once and select the animals for your families and slaughter the Passover lamb. Take a bunch of hyssop, dip it into the blood in the basin and put some of the blood on the top and on both sides of the door-frame. None of you shall go out of the door of your house until morning. When the* Lord *goes through the land to strike down the Egyptians, he will see the blood on the top and sides of the door-frame and will pass over that doorway, and he will not permit the destroyer to enter your houses..."*

Discuss It

- *How many of the plagues can you remember by name? Which one changed Pharaoh's mind?*
- *What did each household have to do to be protected from God's judgment and be set free from slavery in Egypt?*
- *In God's story, who is the ultimate Passover lamb and what did he have to do so that we can be saved?*
- *What do we have to do personally to be protected from God's judgment and be set free from the slavery of sin?*

Pray It

Dear Jesus, thank you for loving us so much that you shed your blood for us. Thank you that through your death on the cross we can be set free. We choose to put our trust in you, our Passover lamb. Amen.

Do It

Go catch a frog and put it in someone's bed!
Or play football blindfolded in the dark.

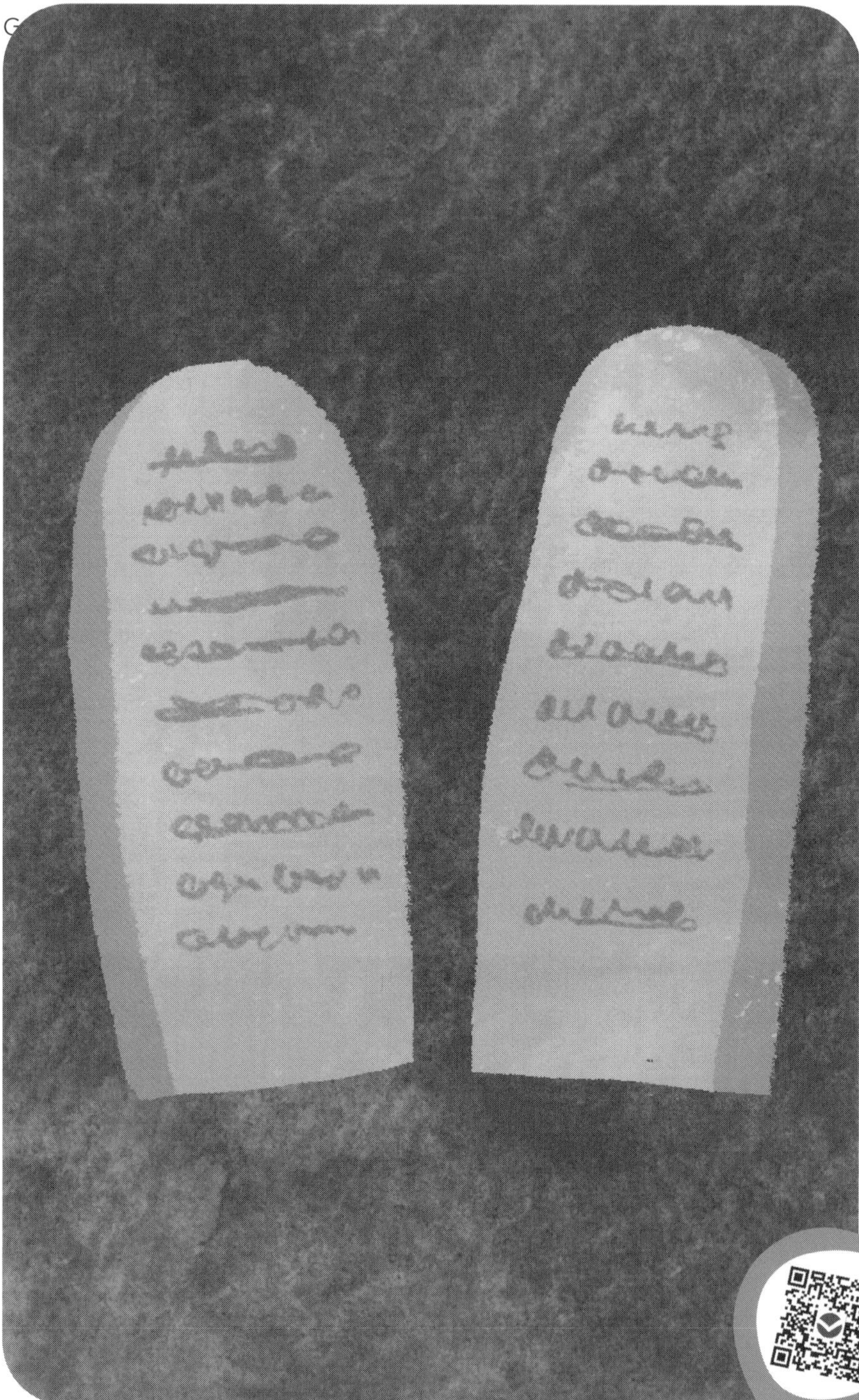

DAY 13

The Law: Ten Commandments

EXODUS 19 – 34

Our Story

What sport or game do you enjoy playing or watching? Name one important rule. What happens if a player breaks that rule?

Imagine playing that game with no rules. Or imagine what would happen if drivers didn't follow the rules of the road. It would cause chaos, and people would get hurt.

God's Story

When Pharaoh finally gave in, Israel got the green light to go. And when Pharaoh changed his mind and chased after them, God opened up a sea and made a way for them to escape. As the waters closed behind them, they were free on the other side. Free from Pharaoh. Exited from Egypt. But what now? God led them through the wilderness in a pillar of cloud in the day and a pillar of fire by night. The nation of Israel was on their way to the beautiful promised land, Canaan. In today's story, we will see how they get on...

The Law Story

The Israelites were not good at remembering. Within days they had forgotten the might and power of God: the plagues, the rescue, the Red Sea parted, the destruction of Pharaoh's army. They had God travelling with them in cloud and fire yet they still asked, "Is the Lord among us or not?" They complained, grumbled, quarrelled and blamed Moses and God for their problems. They simply did not trust God or understand who he was.

They really annoyed Moses. "What am I to do with these people?" he cried.

But God continued to show the Israelites who he was and what he was like. He produced water from a rock and made bitter water sweet. He set up a heavenly meal plan: daily fresh bread and meat for everyone. He gave the Israelites victory when enemies attacked.

"See," God was demonstrating again and again, "I love you. I can and I will protect, care for and provide for you."

Three months after leaving Egypt, the Israelites arrived at Mount Sinai. Here God would tell them how to be his people and how to live well together. He called them to the foot of the mountain. There was an almighty and terrifying display of his power: the mountain shook violently, thick clouds descended, smoke billowed up. There was rumbling and lightning, and thunder and trumpet blasts that got louder and louder and louder.

God summoned Moses to the mountain top to receive a strange gift—ten rules written on stone tablets. Four were about loving God and six were about loving other people. The first commandment? "Worship no god but me."

Now, the Israelites had promised they would do everything the Lord said. But remember, they had poor memories, complained a lot and did not really trust God. So, while God was giving Moses his good laws on top of Mount Sinai, the rest of the Israelites were busy breaking them at the bottom. They actually made a golden calf to worship!

Moses smashed the stones containing the rules the Israelites had broken and destroyed the golden calf. He also pleaded with God to forgive their sins. And because Israel was God's "treasured possession", he gave them not only another copy of his laws but another chance as well.

God's Story

God's people needed commandments to know right from wrong and what would please and displease God. These laws would bring them order, security, health and protection. These laws would keep them close to God, shape their nation's identity and make them holy—more like God than like the nations around. And these laws would show Israel their sin and therefore their need for forgiveness.

The problem was that rules, once broken, cannot save. But the commandments and laws pointed to someone to come who would be totally obedient and keep all God's laws—and who would then choose to save God's people from their sin.

Our Story

Do you know what Jesus said when asked what the most important commandment was? He summed them all up by saying, "Love the Lord your God with all your heart and with all your soul and with all your mind" and "Love your neighbour as yourself". This is a great challenge, but God's Spirit will help us when we ask him; and, because of Jesus, God will forgive us when we need it.

Read It: Exodus 20 v 1-17

God spoke all these words: "I am the LORD your God, who brought you out of Egypt, out of the land of slavery.
"You shall have no other gods before me.
"You shall not make for yourself an image in the form of anything in heaven above or on the earth beneath or in the waters below.
"You shall not bow down to them or worship them
"You shall not misuse the name of the LORD your God
"Remember the Sabbath day by keeping it holy.
"Honour your father and your mother
"You shall not murder.
"You shall not commit adultery.
"You shall not steal.
"You shall not give false testimony against your neighbour.
"You shall not covet."

Discuss It

- *How many of the Ten Commandments can you remember?*
- *Which commandment do you think is the most important?*
- *Imagine if we all kept these commandments. How would the world be a better place?*
- *Which one commandment do you most need to work on keeping?*
- *Why is it good news that Jesus kept the commandments and that he offers forgiveness to those who don't?*

Pray It

Dear God, thank you that your laws are for our good. Please help me especially to keep this commandment [tell God which one]. Help me to put you first and to love other people. Thank you that through Jesus you forgive me when I get things wrong. Amen.

Do It

God wrote the Ten Commandments on stone tablets. Find a rock or pebble and write on it the commandment you are working on.

DAY 14

Joshua: The Promised Land

NUMBERS 13 – 14; JOSHUA 1, 24

Our Story

What are you afraid of? Maybe the dark, spiders, snakes, your teacher, the neighbour's dog, the neighbour?! Is there a big worry for you at the moment? Maybe the future, exams, friendships or family or health? Or as you get older, an interview, money, your boss, housing?

When we are facing a giant problem, we can choose to be full of fear or full of faith. Which do you tend to choose?

God's Story

Today as we rejoin the Bible story, God has rescued his people (now a nation called Israel) from slavery in Egypt and led them through the wilderness to the edge of Canaan. In the Bible this is called the promised land. Twelve spies went in to check it out and came back with a report that left Israel with a choice to make. Would they trust God and his promises or focus on their fears and the problems? Let's imagine Joshua (one of the twelve spies) 40 years later, telling some children all about what happened...

Promised Land Story

"It's a long story. Forty years long. Do you still want to hear it?"

Joshua was warming up his young audience.

"The God of Abraham, Isaac and Jacob promised us a home in Canaan. So, Moses sent me and eleven others to spy out the land. Our exploration was to last 40 days, north and south, 500 miles in all."

"What was it like, Joshua?" asked wide-eyed Hannah.

"It was warm, fertile, green," said Joshua. "Fresh, clear water flowed. The crops were abundant: olives, figs, dates, nuts, melons, pomegranates, grapes—grapes the size of you, children. It took two men to carry the bunch we brought back. It was exceedingly good—a land flowing with milk and honey, like God had said."

"So why did our people not enter this land for 40 years?" interrupted Noah.

"Good question," replied Joshua. "There were some problems that we spied out too. But my friend Caleb and I told Moses and the people, 'We should go up and take possession of the land, for we can certainly do this. The Lord will be with us.'"

"But it was two against ten. The other spies were fearful. They said the people were like giants and the city walls were too high. They said the land would devour us. They compared us to grasshoppers. Overnight, fear swelled in the camp. There was weeping and grumbling. The people doubted. They wouldn't go. They even said the Lord hated them!"

"What did Moses do, Joshua?" asked Hannah.

"More importantly, Hannah," Joshua answered, "what did God do? He called them an 'evil generation, full of contempt'. He refused the adults entry to the land. I've waited 40 years to see today."

"But now we are here!" shouted Eli. "How did you know what to do, Joshua?"

"God said to be strong and courageous and trust him. So we do trust him. You saw what happened when we needed to cross the River Jordan into the land. The priests marched in and the waters instantly stopped flowing and piled up high. Everyone walked over on dry land... You know children, no one will be able to say, 'We did this', for all of us know that God did this. He is with us and we are home... Now, how about some grapes?"

God's Story

God wanted to give the Israelites, his people, a place of beauty, rest and salvation. (A bit like the garden he had made for Adam and Eve.) But fear overwhelmed the people's faith. They focused on the problems, not on the God who promised that he was with them. So they missed out on entering the promised land.

Joshua's name means "the Lord saves". Another form of the same name is Jesus—whose name also means "the Lord saves". He's our Joshua. He also wants to lead us into rest and salvation. If we trust him, he will lead us into an eternal promised land, heaven.

Our Story

Most of the spies and Israelites focused on their fears and the giant problem before them. They did not trust God. Joshua and Caleb focused on their God and his presence with them. Whatever you are afraid of and worried about today, God is with you. Do not fear. As Caleb said, *The Lord is with us; we can certainly do this!*

Read It: Numbers 14 v 6-9

> *Joshua son of Nun and Caleb son of Jephunneh, who were among those who had explored the land, tore their clothes and said to the entire Israelite assembly, "The land we passed through and explored is exceedingly good. If the* Lord *is pleased with us, he will lead us into that land, a land flowing with milk and honey, and will give it to us. Only do not rebel against the* Lord*. And do not be afraid of the people of the land, because we will devour them. Their protection is gone, but the* Lord *is with us. Do not be afraid of them."*

Discuss It

- *What were the names of the two out of the twelve spies who trusted God and said that with his help they could enter the land?*
- *Are you more like Caleb and Joshua who believed, or the ten other spies who said "We can't do this" and wanted to run away?*
- *What situations make you feel nervous and intimidated?*
- *How can fear and worry stop us living a full life if we let them take over?*
- *Why is life so much better if we put our confidence in God and step out in faith?*

Pray It

Dear God, thank you that you are bigger than all my worries and you promise to be with me. I put my confidence in you. Help me not to give in to fear but to step out in faith. Amen.

Do It

Memorise Joshua's words and say them whenever you're intimidated: "The Lord is with us. Do not be afraid" (Numbers 14 v 9)

DAY 15

Memory Verse

"I have come down to rescue them ... and to bring them ... into a good and spacious land."

EXODUS 3 v 8

VERSE-MEMORISING TOP TIPS

Write It

Visualise It

Act It

Sing It

Record It

Use an App

... and repeat, repeat, repeat!

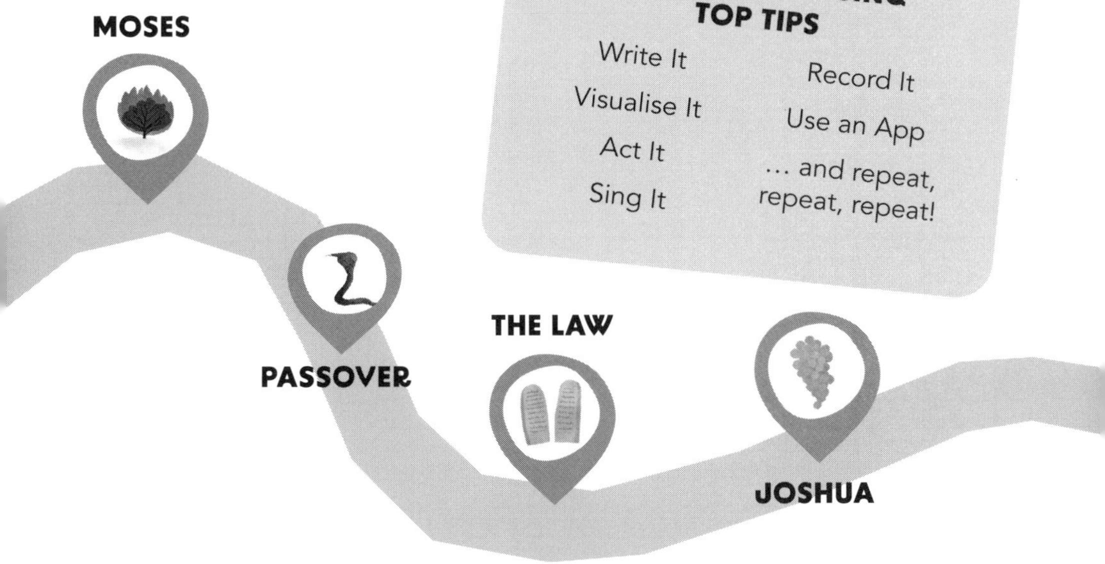

Week Four

Leaders

DAY 16

Gideon: Israel Gets Stuck

JUDGES 6 – 8

Our Story

Have you got any bad habits? Maybe you bite your nails or pick your nose? Maybe you whine, argue or interrupt? (If you're not sure, just ask a family member!) No matter what you do, you just can't seem to break the negative cycle of behaviour. You feel stuck. Well, you are not alone!

God's Story

The Israelites have now settled in to the promised land that God gave them. However, they have got into some seriously bad habits. (Much worse than snoring or being messy.) For 350 years, Israel go through this negative cycle: they forget God, things go badly, they cry out to God, he sends warrior leaders (called judges) to rescue them, they turn back to God, but then they forget him—and round we go again. God's people are stuck in the bad habit of forgetting God every time things are going okay. In the middle of this period, God's people are suffering under the Midianites…

Gideon's Story

God's people, petrified and poor, were hiding in caves. Their crops, animals and lives had been ruined by their enemies, the Midianites, and after seven desperate years they cried out to God.

God loved them. So he visited Gideon.

Gideon was puny.

Gideon was scared.

Gideon (bizarrely) was sorting out wheat in a winepress.

(Trust me, this was an odd thing to do, but he needed to hide.)

God's message was clear: God was with Gideon, and he would defeat the Midianites...

But first Gideon must challenge Israel's idol worship by destroying his family's homemade fake gods. Puny, scared and under the cover of darkness, Gideon obediently did what God asked. He chopped down their Asherah pole and smashed up the fake god Baal's altar, and replaced them with a worship space to God.

God's Spirit fell on Gideon—but he still felt puny and scared, so he asked God for a sign. Could his rug be soaked with dew but the ground be dry? Then, could his rug stay dry while the ground was wet? Only God could do this. And he did!

Gideon's faith rose. He summoned five clans of fighting men, 32,000 in all. But God said, "Too many. Those who are scared should go home." 20,000 fled. "Still too many!" God said again. "The ones who drank water at the river by lapping it like dogs... they can leave too!"

Only 300 Israelites remained.

Meanwhile, 135,000 Midianites crossed the Jordan and set up camp. Their military might, their camels and iron swords were waiting, and they were deadly.

In comparison, Gideon's 300 men and weird battle strategy seemed disastrous. But what had God said?

"The Lord is with you, mighty warrior.
Go in the strength that you have.
You will strike down all the Midianites.
With three hundred men I will save you."

Gideon believed. Gideon obeyed.

They crept down to the camp in darkness. Blew their trumpets. Smashed their jars. Held their torches aloft and shouted, "A sword for the Lord and for Gideon." (Even though, bizarrely, they had no swords.) All the Midianites, thrown into confusion, fled or struck each other down.

You see, Gideon didn't need military might or cutting-edge battle technology. He and his tiny army needed only faith, torches and trumpets. God did the rest.

God's Story

Israel needed leaders who trusted God and could get them out of the mess they were in. God knows that we need a leader too. Not just a warrior leader who will battle armies but a once-for-all-leader; a leader who has won the biggest battles, against sin, sickness and even death. A leader who will rule and be the Lord at the same time. Any ideas who that might be?!

Our Story

The Israelites forgot God. At the end of the book of Judges it says that everyone did what was right in their own eyes. Can you imagine? Like the Israelites, if we forget God we can get stuck in negative behaviours and thinking too. That's why we also need God's rescue. Then we must commit to keep worshipping him, gathering with his people, and reading the Bible and putting it into practice. The good news is that God's Spirit who came on Gideon lives in all of Jesus' people today, and he can help you break bad habits of not trusting and obeying God, and help you live bravely for him too!

Read It: Judges 6 v 11-12, 14

> *The angel of the LORD came and sat down under the oak in Ophrah that belonged to Joash the Abiezrite, where his son Gideon was threshing wheat in a winepress to keep it from the Midianites. When the angel of the LORD appeared to Gideon, he said, "The LORD is with you, mighty warrior." ...*
>
> *The LORD turned to him and said, "Go in the strength you have and save Israel out of Midian's hand. Am I not sending you?"*

Discuss It

- *What were the consequences of Israel forgetting the wonderful things God had done for them?*
- *What three things did God tell Gideon's army to take into battle?*
- *If you were going to fight a battle, what three things would you take with you?*
- *What was the big lesson God wanted Gideon and his army to learn?*

Pray It

Dear God, thank you that you never forget me. Sorry when I forget you. Help me get in the habit of remembering the wonderful things you have done and staying close to you. Amen.

Do It

What are some of the wonderful things God has done for you? Put a note in your pocket or a reminder somewhere to remember to thank God for the wonderful things he's done.

DAY 17

Ruth: Joining God's Family

RUTH 1 – 4

Our Story

The hero of today's story is loyal when things get really tough. Her name, Ruth, means "friend". Can you think of a friend who has stuck with you when things have been tough? How do you think it would feel to know you always had a friend like that?

God's Story

The story of Ruth is set in the time of the judges—leaders like Gideon, who we looked at last time. By now, God's people, Israel, have been living in the promised land for years. But they're in a mess again, serving false gods and facing hard times.

Ruth's Story

Israel had no water. Israel had no food. And people began to starve. So, Naomi's family moved away from Bethlehem, away from the promised land, to another country, Moab. (Now, be sure to understand that Moab was enemy territory. The Israelites *hated* the Moabites.)

Naomi's move to Moab ended in disaster. Her husband got sick and died, and so did her sons. So Naomi decided to return home. However, one of her sons had married a local girl from Moab, called Ruth. When Naomi was leaving for Bethlehem, Ruth stuck to her like a magnet, even though Naomi insisted she should stay. "Where you go I will go," Ruth said. "Your people will be my people and your God my God."

When they arrived in Bethlehem, it was harvest time. There was water! There was food! But Ruth and Naomi had no land, so they had no food—and they had no one to protect them. As Naomi met old friends, she told them to call her Mara, meaning bitter, because her life had been so hard.

Although it was risky, Ruth decided she must go into the fields to gather leftover grain so they could eat. But which field? There were so many! She needed a field of kindness, owned by someone who followed God's laws, where a generous amount was left behind by the harvesters for the poor, the foreigners and the widows to collect. She needed a field where the men would not bother, upset or hurt her...

Surely Ruth was praying as she entered a field and started to collect the barley. Surely Naomi was praying too as she waited for Ruth to come back.

Ruth worked hard, and Ruth got noticed...

Now as it so happened, this field belonged to a wealthy and compassionate man, Boaz. This kind farmer insisted that Ruth work in his fields until all the harvesting was done. He told his servants to keep her safe. He commanded them to drop extra grain in her way.

Imagine Naomi's joy as Ruth arrived home safely with bundles of food.

Imagine Naomi's amazement when she heard about Boaz. Ruth had just happened to wander into the field of one of Naomi's distant relatives. What a coincidence! (Well it looked like a coincidence—but of course people were praying and God was still at work on his rescue plan!) Would God use Boaz to protect them both, rescue them from poverty and provide for their needs? In other words, would God use Boaz as their "redeemer". Yes he would....

God's Story

Ruth continued to return to the field until the harvesting was over. Before long, Ruth and Boaz got married. They had a son called Obed, and Obed was grandfather to King David. (We'll get to him shortly.) Centuries later, a famous relative of King David was also born in Bethlehem. Can you guess who?!

Despite all her pain, Naomi's life finished sweet, not bitter, because of her faithful friend Ruth and her redeemer Boaz.

Our Story

Like Ruth, we can become part of God's amazing family. We enter it through trusting and following Jesus.

Like Boaz, Jesus is our Rescuer and Redeemer. He takes care of us and provides all we need. He is the perfect friend who will never let us down.

Read It: Ruth 1 v 16; 4 v 13-17

Ruth replied [to Naomi], "Don't urge me to leave you or to turn back from you. Where you go I will go, and where you stay I will stay. Your people will be my people and your God my God." ...

So Boaz took Ruth and she became his wife. When he made love to her, the Lord enabled her to conceive, and she gave birth to a son. The women said to Naomi: 'Praise be to the LORD" ...

Then Naomi took the child in her arms and cared for him. ... And they named him Obed. He was the father of Jesse, the father of David.

Discuss It

- *Where have you heard about Bethlehem before? Hold onto that thought!*
- *Ruth wasn't part of God's chosen family but in this story she travels to Bethlehem in Israel. Why?*
- *Who looked after them when they arrived in Bethlehem? How? Why?*
- *How does what Boaz did for Ruth show what Jesus can do for us?*
- *Why was Ruth a very unlikely person to be included into God's people? And what does that tell us about who can join God's people today?*

Pray It

Dear God, thank you for your rescue, protection and care. Thank you that through Jesus I can be redeemed and brought into your family. Help me to be a friend who is as loyal as Ruth and as generous as Boaz. Amen.

Do It

Do something kind and generous for a friend today.

DAY 18

King David: A Heart for God

1 SAMUEL 16 – 17

Our Story

Are there things wrong with your community or the world that make you feel unhappy or even angry? Maybe an environmental issue? Racism? A bully?

Maybe you feel you are too young to do anything about it. Consider, however, the humble female mosquito: 6mm long and living for six weeks, her buzz may keep you up at night but her bite could give you a nasty bump or even a deadly disease. Very small things can have a humongous impact.

God's Story

After the time of the judges, Israel decided they didn't want God as their King. They wanted a king in person, a big strong king they could see, just like the nations around them. But Saul, their big, strong first king, disobeyed God. In today's story, it's time to choose a new one, and God gives Israel the king they need rather than the king they want.

David's Story

Judge Samuel set off for Bethlehem. His mission? To choose a future king, one of Jesse's sons. The oldest was tall, muscular and handsome. "He looks like a king", thought Samuel. "He's the one!"

"No, he's not", said God.

Samuel met six more sons. "Not him either", God whispered to Samuel. "Nor him… nor him… nor him. You are looking at the outside… but I look at the heart."

"Got any more sons?" Samuel asked Jesse.

"My eighth, the youngest, is out with the sheep..." he said.

The smallest arrived. Smelly and grassy. Handsome and healthy, with twinkly eyes.

The Lord said, "He is the one. His heart is like mine."

And when Samuel poured anointing oil on David's head, God's Spirit immediately filled him and stayed with him.

Mission accomplished—a new king had been anointed.

Some time later, David set out from Bethlehem. His mission (or so he thought) was to get cheese sandwiches to his brothers on the frontline of Israel's battle with the Philistines. As he arrived, a nine-foot giant tank of a man emerged from the Philistine ranks and issued an outrageous challenge to Israel and their God...

"One of you—come fight me! If you kill me, we will become your slaves, but if I kill you, you will all become our slaves."

"How dare this Philistine be so rude and ignorant about our God and his army?" seethed David. "Has King Saul not stood up to Goliath? What about our mightiest men or our most skilled soldiers?"

Trembling, as they had for 40 days, no one answered, but they took David to see Saul.

"Though I'm a boy, I am able, I'll take him on," said David. "I've saved sheep from lions. This giant is the same, but worse, because he belittles and ridicules our God! I don't need armour. God has protected me against bears. He'll protect me today."

David set off towards Goliath. His new mission? To slay a giant and show that the Lord saves.

"You're only a boy!" sneered Goliath.

"You have no idea that you've picked a fight with the living God!" laughed David.

Running, David took a stone and slung it, striking Goliath on the head.

Boom! The giant crashed to the ground.

When they saw their hero and champion dead, the Philistines fled.

Two missions accomplished—cheese sandwiches delivered and one giant ungodly problem resolved.

God's Story

God sent David as a saviour from Bethlehem to rescue his people. But after David killed Goliath, Saul was jealous and made life tough for David. When Saul died, David finally became king and reigned for 40 years. Even though David made some big mistakes (most of all, stealing another man's wife and having that man killed), the Bible says he was a man after God's heart. He was the best king Israel ever had.

David points towards Jesus, the very best Shepherd, King and Saviour, who never made mistakes. Jesus did not fight human giants. His battle was with our greatest enemies: Satan, sin and death. Like David, Jesus won a great victory against the odds, through his death on the cross.

Our Story

David did not see himself as "only a boy" but as someone who could do anything because God was with him. No one is too small to be on God's team. No one is too young to be filled with God's Spirit. When we trust God, even though we're small we can make a humungous difference for him. We can face tough challenges, knowing he is with us.

Read It: 1 Samuel 16 v 6-7, 12-13

> *When they arrived, Samuel saw Eliab and thought, "Surely the LORD's anointed stands here before the LORD."*
>
> *But the LORD said to Samuel, "Do not consider his appearance or his height, for I have rejected him. The LORD does not look at the things people look at. People look at the outward appearance, but the LORD looks at the heart." …*
>
> *[David] was glowing with health and had a fine appearance and handsome features.*
>
> *Then the LORD said, "Rise and anoint him; this is the one."*
>
> *So Samuel took the horn of oil and anointed him in the presence of his brothers, and from that day on the Spirit of the LORD came powerfully upon David.*

Discuss It

- *Why did God choose David to be the next king?*
- *What gave David the confidence to stand up to Goliath?*
- *What challenges do we need the Holy Spirit to help us with at the moment?*
- *What would it look like for us to be people "after God's heart"?*

Pray It

Dear God, thank you that you don't judge us by how we look. Give each of us a heart that is like yours and the ability to love others as you do. Please give us the help of your Holy Spirit to face our Goliath-size challenges. All our confidence is in you. Amen.

Do It

Go look in the mirror and tell yourself, "God's more concerned about my heart than my hair!"

DAY 19

Solomon's Temple: A Home for God

1 KINGS 3 – 10

Our Story

What is the most impressive building you have been in? Maybe a football stadium or concert venue? A castle or temple? Sometimes it's not only the building that is amazing—the person who built it or lives there may be remarkable too.

God's Story

Today's story features an incredible building, but it's the person who comes to live there that's most impressive of all. You might remember that for many years after the Exodus, the Israelites moved around, camping in the wilderness. And as they did so, God moved with them, dwelling in a special tent he told them to make for him, called the tabernacle.

By now, 480 years after leaving Egypt, God's promises to Abraham are coming true. There are many Israelite people, they live in peace in a beautiful land, and they are ruled by God's king. King David had made Jerusalem a permanent capital city and he wanted to build God a permanent home there too. However, because David was a warrior, God only gave him the building plans. Today's story is about how God gave the temple project to David's son, King Solomon.

Temple Story

One night, just after Solomon became king, God visited him in a dream and asked him what he wanted. His reply was incredible: "I ... do not know how to carry out my duties ... give your servant a discerning heart to govern your people and to distinguish right from wrong." God thought this was a first-class request. So he made Solomon not just the wisest but also the richest king ever!

Israel was a safe and happy place. Silver was as common as stones! It was definitely time to build a home for God. Plans, people and particulars were sorted.

80,000 stonemasons, 30,000 lumberjacks and 3,300 foremen were employed. Large expensive foundation stones were hewn: olive wood, cedar and juniper wood was felled. Gold chains, lampstands, plates and nails were crafted. Pomegranates, gourds, palm trees, cherubim and flowers were carved. Pure gold and jewels lined the walls.

It took seven years for God's home to be built. It stood four floors high, 27 metres long and nine metres wide. (That's half an Olympic-size swimming pool, or a whole basketball court.) Up on the Jerusalem hill it could be seen for miles. It was the biggest, snazziest, shiniest temple ever.

Solomon invited the elders, priests and people to the opening. The whole nation came. Huge sacrifices were offered. The ark of the covenant—the special golden box that had been the place God dwelled right in the middle of the tabernacle—was brought in, and Solomon prayed, kneeling, with his hands spread out in worship towards heaven...

And God arrived! His presence was made visible in the form of a cloud. His presence was so strong that the priests could not perform their duties, for his glory filled his temple.

God promised that day, "My eyes and my heart will always be here".

Solomon was now world famous. Even the amazingly wealthy Queen of Sheba was overwhelmed by his wisdom and wealth when she visited. She praised God—and so did God's people. It was the safest, happiest and greatest time in Israel's history.

God's Story

The most special thing about the temple was not its size or design—it was that God lived there. Solomon couldn't quite believe this, and when the temple was finished he asked, "But will God really dwell on earth?" Notice however that God came and took up residence in the temple only after the sacrifices had been made. Note too that God can only come and take up residence in our lives because of the sacrifice Jesus made on the cross.

Our Story

Solomon's life is a wonderful example to us all—but it is also a warning. Like his father David, Solomon made seriously poor choices as he grew older. A good start is great—but we need to finish what we started too.

It's wonderful that we don't need to visit a special temple or building to meet with God anymore. When we believe in Jesus, we become mini-temples as God's Spirit comes to live in us. What a privilege! We can host God's royal presence. He's with us wherever we go.

Read It: 2 Chronicles 5 v 1, 13-14

When all the work Solomon had done for the temple of the LORD was finished, he brought in the things his father David had dedicated—the silver and gold and all the furnishings—and he placed them in the treasuries of God's temple …

The trumpeters and musicians joined in unison to give praise and thanks to the LORD. Accompanied by trumpets, cymbals and other instruments, the singers raised their voices in praise to the LORD and sang:

"He is good;
his love endures for ever."

Then the temple of the LORD was filled with the cloud, and the priests could not perform their service because of the cloud, for the glory of the LORD filled the temple of God.

Discuss It

- *If you could ask God for anything, what would you ask for?*
- *What did Solomon ask for and what did God also give him?*
- *Who came to live in the massive, beautiful building Solomon built?*
- *Why do we not need to go to a special building to meet with God today?*
- *How do you think we can be good hosts of God's presence and worship him today?*

Pray It

Dear God, thank you for your plan to come and live with your people. Thank you that we don't have to visit a temple anymore to worship you; thank you that, because of Jesus' sacrifice, you can live in each of us by your Spirit. Help us to host you well today, and every day of our lives. Amen.

Do It

At your next family meal, set an extra place as a reminder that you are hosting the presence of God.

DAY 20

Memory Verse

"People look at the outward appearance, but the Lord looks at the heart."

1 SAMUEL 16 v 7

VERSE-MEMORISING TOP TIPS

Write It
Visualise It
Act It
Sing It
Record It
Use an App
... and repeat, repeat, repeat!

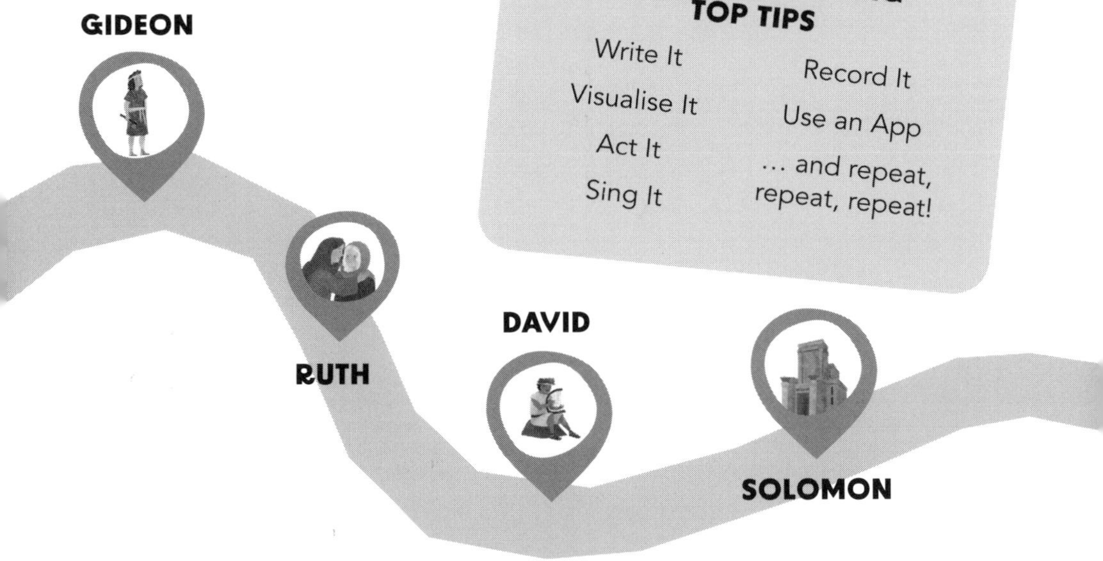

Week Five

Messengers

DAY 21

Elijah: The Lord Is God

1 KINGS 17 – 18

Our Story

What is the most important message you have ever received? You're getting a puppy, or a new baby brother or sister? You won the league? You passed?! Or maybe it's something more serious, like you have to go and see your teacher about that thing that happened in the playground?

God's Story

In today's story, Elijah has a vital message for God's people. After King Solomon's time, God's people divided into two kingdoms. They fought each other and they continued to worship homemade gods. Worship of the fake god Baal, who people said controlled the weather, was so normal that it became the official religion. Under King Ahab and Queen Jezebel, God's people in the northern kingdom almost totally forgot God. (The Bible says Ahab was so evil he made God angry.) They were in a mess. They needed to hear God's voice.

Elijah's Story

Striding towards evil Ahab's throne, Elijah announced, "As surely as the Lord, the God of Israel lives, whom I serve, there will be neither dew nor rain in the next few years except by my word." What a challenge to Ahab and Jezebel, and their weather god, Baal! They were about to discover who really was the master of the rain and the Lord of life.

Fleeing many miles and hiding in the Cherith Valley, as the Lord had told him to, Elijah waited for the ravens. Morning and night these scavengers brought bread and meat from the wilderness. He drank from the small brook—until that dried up too.

Three years went by. Elijah returned to the king. "Trouble maker of Israel! Bringer of drought, death and disaster!" Ahab roared.

"Your trust in Baal and your evil influence on God's people brought this trouble, not me," Elijah replied. "Now, bring the people and your prophets. Meet me on the mountain where you love worshipping Baal. There the real god will show himself."

Gathering the people on Mount Carmel, Elijah challenged them, "If the LORD is God, follow him; but if Baal is god, follow him."

To the 450 prophets of Baal, Elijah said, "Build an altar, sacrifice a bull and ask your master, Baal, to send fire."

So they did. They spent hours... Praying. Pleading. Prancing. Nothing happened.

Elijah began teasing. "I'd shout louder if I were you. Maybe Baal is asleep, or on holiday, or maybe he's on the toilet?!"

So they spent more hours... Shouting. Slashing. Screaming.

There was no response. No one answered. No one paid any attention.

Elijah was taunting: "Perhaps Baal is deaf?"

Exhausting. Embarrassing. Annoying. Nothing. Not a thing all day.

Elijah gathered twelve stones. Built an altar. Drowned it in water. Piled on wood. Placed the bull on top.

All the people were... Watching. Waiting. Wondering...

"Is the LORD the real God?"

Then Elijah prayed.

"LORD God, show that you are the God of Israel. Show these people who you are, so they will follow you again."

Fire from the Lord fell from heaven onto the altar.

Scorching, searing, sizzling. Burning, bursting, baking...

There was nothing left. No bull, wood, stones or water.

Now there were... Cheering voices. Changing hearts. Choosing minds.

"The LORD, he is God!"

And, as Elijah looked, there were... Blackening skies. Burgeoning clouds. Bucketing rain.

And frightened, finished, false prophets and a furious king and queen.

God's Story

God showed his people again that he is the real God—the master of the weather, the ravens, life and death. He alone gives life, not the homemade god, Baal. The people on Mount Carmel that day had no doubt that the Lord was God.

Our Story

Elijah's challenge to the people is the same challenge for us today. What do we put our trust in and who do we depend on? As Elijah said, "If the LORD is God, follow him". On another mountain in Jerusalem, 800 years later, another challenge was set out. When he rose from the dead, Jesus showed that he is the Lord of life and more powerful than death, evil and all the made-up gods. In response to God's display of power in bringing Jesus back to life, who will you choose to follow?

Read It: 1 Kings 17 v 1; 18 v 20-21

> *Elijah the Tishbite, from Tishbe in Gilead, said to Ahab, "As the LORD, the God of Israel, lives, whom I serve, there will be neither dew nor rain in the next few years except at my word."* *[Three years later...]*
>
> *Ahab sent word throughout all Israel and assembled the prophets on Mount Carmel. Elijah went before the people and said, "How long will you waver between two opinions? If the LORD is God, follow him; but if Baal is God, follow him." But the people said nothing.*

Discuss It

- *What is the most surprising message you have ever received?*
- *How did what happened on Mount Carmel prove that the God who Elijah worshipped was the only true God?*
- *Just like the people in Elijah's time, sometimes we put our trust in the wrong things to give us what we need or make us happy. If Elijah were around today, what things do you think he would challenge us about?*
- *In response to God's display of power in bringing Jesus back to life, what do you say? Do you think this shows he is the Lord of life?*

Pray It

Dear God, we believe you are the true and living God. Sorry for trusting in other things. Help us to trust you, see your power at work and follow you with all our hearts. Amen.

Do It

Turn the tap on. Thank God for water. Shout three times, "The Lord is God. We worship him!"

DAY 22

Jonah: Go God's Way

JONAH 1 – 4

Our Story

Have you ever been told to do something but you disobeyed and did something else? Maybe you were asked to buy milk, and you bought chocolate ? Or to tidy your room, but you had a snooze? Or to do your online maths homework but you sneaked in watching some YouTube reels?

God's Story

In today's story we are going to read about Jonah. He lived near Nazareth and had a different task to God's other messengers. He had to go outside Israel to the city of Nineveh, the capital of the Assyrian Empire, with a message of change. Jonah wasn't happy about this. Assyria was not only a foreign nation but Israel's enemy and aggressor. Surely the God who loved Israel wouldn't send his messenger to their enemies?

Jonah's Story

This mission wasn't for me. Our sworn enemies, the Assyrians, should not get the chance to experience God's love. Plus, they could have made me into dog food, or worse, actually listened. So, I decided to sail west to Spain rather than east to Nineveh.

Incredibly, a boat was just there... I had just the right money... The sea was calm...

I hopped aboard.

Running away from my mission and from God left me exhausted. I lay in my bunk and snored, I was blissfully unaware of the violent storm, petrified prayers and tossing of cargo overboard. I was, however, acutely aware of the captain's bellowing, "What have you done? Get up and call on your god!"

My plan for a sunny stay in Spain was looking less certain...

"It's my fault," I confessed. "Throw me overboard." So the sailors did.

Thankfully, God did not have death by drowning in mind, but rescue by whale. It was just rounding the corner as I splashed down...

Inside was cavernous, slimy and fishy-smelling. Those three days sure did make me think, and then being upchucked on a beach was an experience! As I lay, covered in fish vomit, God returned me to my mission. "Go, Jonah. Preach against Nineveh."

Fish goo hadn't improved my trendy preacher-boy image but this time I went. I challenged 120,000 Assyrians about their sin and their need to change. Doing that *with* God was better than being inside a whale *without* him...

Nineveh is awesome; the largest city in the world, the capital of the empire, with royal palaces, temples, thick fortified walls. It took me three days to walk it all.

My message was punchy. "Forty days. Stop your wickedness, or God will destroy you." The king heard and commanded everyone to fast and pray. And do you know what? Those stinking Assyrians actually listened! God gave those undeserving, not-of-his-promise people his forgiveness and love. I was incensed. I wanted to die.

But God had compassion on me too. He'd provided a storm and a vomiting fish. He now gave me some sound reasoning and forgiveness. Oh, and a worm, to destroy my shady vine and remind me that people are much more important than plants and that God's love is for all nations.

I'm still feeling kinda grumpy. But when God next says, "Go!" I'll not be so slow. Salvation comes from the Lord!

God's Story

Jonah understandably felt upset that he had to go and tell his enemies, the people who had attacked and destroyed Israel, that God was angry with them and they needed to change and be forgiven. He wasn't concerned for them and he didn't understand the promises given to Abraham. Do you recall them? God was going to use this family, the Israelites—including Jonah—to bless all people and nations. Even the Assyrians.

Jonah's preaching is a picture of what Jesus would do. He would bring all people to God. In fact he called himself the one "greater than Jonah" (Matthew 12 v 41).

120,000 people turned to God and found forgiveness after Jonah's three days and nights in the fish. Millions more have found forgiveness through the one who spent three days and nights in death—and then rose again.

Our Story

The story of Jonah is a big challenge to us. All of us are equally undeserving of forgiveness and a relationship with God. And all of us have people we dislike—maybe even some whom we would consider an enemy. But God loves those people and wants them to find him. And he wants us to pray for them, and to show and tell them about his love.

Read It: Jonah 1 v 1-3; 2 v 10 – 3 v 2

> *The word of the LORD came to Jonah son of Amittai: "Go to the great city of Nineveh and preach against it, because its wickedness has come up before me." But Jonah ran away from the Lord and headed for Tarshish. He went down to Joppa, where he found a ship bound for that port. After paying the fare, he went aboard and sailed for Tarshish to flee from the LORD.*

> *[Three days later...] The LORD commanded the fish, and it vomited Jonah onto dry land. Then the word of the LORD came to Jonah a second time: "Go to the great city of Nineveh and proclaim to it the message I give you."*

Discuss It

- *Have you ever done the total opposite of what someone asked you to do? Why?*
- *What things did God use to get Jonah to go to Nineveh?*
- *In what ways do we avoid doing what God asks us to do?*
- *It's challenging, but how can we share the good news message about Jesus this week with others?*

Pray It

Dear God, thank you for always giving me a second chance. Forgive me for the times I have run away from doing the things you wanted me to do. Help me to be brave and to bring your message of good news to the people around me today. Amen.

Do It

Share some good news about God with a friend or someone in your family (via text, Snapchat, WhatsApp... or, better, talking on the phone or face to face!).

DAY 23

Huldah: Follow God's Word

2 KINGS 21 – 23

Our Story

Imagine you were a king or queen for a day. What would you do? Maybe you would wear royal robes and parade around in a carriage. Maybe you would eat ice-cream for breakfast in the tower of your favourite castle. Or maybe you would invite the poor in for a picnic?

God's Story

In today's story we will see again how much God's people depend on the king paying attention to God's word. It's 600 years before Jesus. Many prophets have brought challenges, warnings and encouragements to the kings but nothing works for long. The people flip-flop between following God and wandering far away from him. In today's story we will meet a little known lady messenger who encourages the king, Josiah, to continue in radical obedience to God's word.

Huldah's Story

My name is Huldah. (Bet you've not heard that name before?!) I live in Jerusalem, between the first and second walls, near the palace and temple. My husband, Shallum, works for the king, looking after his clothes.

I'm different. I'm one of the few who follow God, and I'm a prophetess. (Prophecy is normally a job for men.) So I was rather shocked by THE VISIT that day from the king's courtiers.

This all started not with our king, Josiah, but with his wicked grandad, Manasseh. For 55 years, Manasseh led God's people into great evil; he was a sorcerer who sacrificed his children to his gods, slaughtered innocent people and worshipped the stars, placing altars to them in God's temple. His son, Amnon, reigned for two years. Then his son, Josiah, aged only eight, inherited a kingdom in crisis. This was 18 years ago.

I watched Josiah prayerfully. He was different. At 16, he sought God. At 20, he rid the nation of idolatry, grinding up homemade gods and smashing ungodly altars. At 26, he repaired our ramshackle temple.

Here a discovery was made. Hilkiah, the high priest, found a scroll, hidden away, squashed and dusty but legible—a whole book full of God's words. He took it to Shaphan, the secretary, who took it and read it to King Josiah—who, when he heard it, wept and tore his clothes (much to my husband's displeasure). Why? Josiah was overcome with how little he understood and how far we had drifted from God.

Hence, THE VISIT!

The king charged his five leading men to "enquire of the Lord ... about what was written in this book". However, they didn't know how, so they visited me. They knew I would not edit or sweeten God's message for anyone—whether priest or peasant, king or country. So, with wisdom and authority from God, I confirmed that this was God's book and it must be respected and followed.

And in obedience to God, I prophesied that because his people had turned away from him, God would destroy Judah and Jerusalem. However, because Josiah honoured God's word, he would see peace.

Josiah's response was radical. He summoned everyone—not just the priests—to the temple. We all, from the least to the greatest, heard God's words for the first time, read by the king himself.

He is calling the nation back to God. He is doing what God's word says.

God's Story

Huldah respected and honoured God's book—what we now call the Bible (though of course, they only had part of the Old Testament back then). God is looking for people who read his words, do what they say, listen to his voice and pass his message on. King Josiah, like Huldah, did exactly what God's word said, even when it was not popular or normal. He changed a nation because he obeyed what God said.

Our Story

Where do you keep your Bible? Is it hidden away, squashed and dusty, or do you read it often and keep it in a place where you can grab it at any time? When you read it, remember it is God speaking through these words and it is written for you. Think about what it tells you about God and the way he wants you to live. Do what it says! Honouring and trusting God's word can transform you, your family and your community in amazing ways.

Read It: 2 Kings 23 v 1-3

Then the king called together all the elders of Judah and Jerusalem. He went up to the temple of the LORD with the people of Judah, the inhabitants of Jerusalem, the priests and the prophets—all the people from the least to the greatest. He read in their hearing all the words of the Book of the Covenant, which had been found in the temple of the LORD. The king stood by the pillar and renewed the covenant in the presence of the LORD—to follow the LORD and keep his commands, statutes and decrees with all his heart and all his soul, thus confirming the words of the covenant written in this book. Then all the people pledged themselves to the covenant.

Discuss It

- *After God's book was found in the temple, what did Josiah do and what did Huldah say?*
- *Have you ever changed something about the way you do things because of what you've read in the Bible?*
- *How do you feel about reading your Bible?*
- *Have you heard anything from Huldah and Josiah's story that has changed your view in any way?*

Pray It

Dear God, thank you for the Bible. Thank you for all the things you teach us through it. Help us to be like the prophet Huldah who understood it and King Josiah who bravely put it into practice. Amen.

Do It

How quickly can you grab your Bible now? Do you know where it is? You may have more than one Bible in your house. Time yourselves to see how long it takes to collect all of them up. Hopefully they are not lost, squashed or dusty?

On your marks, get set, GO!

DAY 24

Jeremiah: Help the Poor

THE BOOK OF JEREMIAH

Our Story

What do you want to do when you grow up? Marry your teacher?—ha! Fly to Mars?—more likely! Or perhaps be a software engineer, make loads of money, or follow in your parent's profession?

God's Story

Today's story is about Jeremiah. He was expected to be a priest and live up north, like his dad. However, God had other plans. Jeremiah ended up living down south in Jerusalem and became God's messenger, like Elijah, Jonah and Huldah. He challenged people to be "just"—to care about justice. Do you know what "justice" means? It's about individuals and communities being fair, and the poor and vulnerable being taken care of.

Jeremiah's Story

I was young when God reached out his hand and touched my mouth. Imagine that! He said, "I have put my words in your mouth. See, today, I appoint you as my messenger. Do not be afraid of them. I am with you."

I've prophesied for 40 years, supported King Josiah as he transformed the country, and warned and encouraged his sons, Kings Jehoiakim and Zedekiah. It has not been easy. I've been beaten up, starved, imprisoned, thrown down a well, rescued by dirty laundry and called a liar and a traitor.

I've done crazy stuff—I've hidden my belt under a rock for three years, and then dug it up. And what was God's message? To show his people what it looks like to be destroyed. I bought a clay jar and smashed it in front of Israel's leaders. God's message? "I will smash this nation, just as this potter's jar is smashed."

Yes, I preached like Huldah against homemade gods, but God gave me another message too. Care for the weak! Be concerned for the poor! Early on God challenged me to find people who were truly concerned about justice. How many do you think I found? Two hundred? Twenty? Two?... Not even one! Not one person was concerned for the needy! Then God told me to preach in the temple and remind his people that offering sacrifices wasn't enough. Worship and kindness are partners. You cannot ignore the poor and expect God to be pleased and all to go well.

You know, our God cares for the weak. And the king of God's people should be compassionate and care about justice, just like our God. So I visited King Jehoiakim. I warned him that God was angry because he paid his builders the meanest wages ever. He exploited rather than protected his people. He killed the innocent and crushed the weak.

He didn't listen.

In the end, just as I warned, disobedience and injustice have led to disaster Jerusalem has been burned by the Babylonians. The king's eyes have been plucked out. His sons have been killed. Most of the best people have been carried away to Babylon. But when the leaders say, "We will not listen to the message you have spoken to us in the name of the Lord", what do you expect?

God's Story

So, Jerusalem was ruined like Jeremiah's smashed pot and belt, and God's people were led into exile in Babylon, far away from the land God had promised Abraham and his family. However, God promised hope through Jeremiah too. His people would return and rebuild. And his promised Saviour, that serpent-crushing great King, would still come. But when he did, he would challenge injustice and display care for everyone—especially the poor and vulnerable. Because God's true and perfect King really does care about justice—and he wants his people to do so too.

Our Story

Worshipping God includes taking care of the poor and vulnerable. We tend to focus on the world's idea of success—making lots of money or having a very good job. God may have another idea for your life...

We tend also to look after ourselves rather than thinking about the poor and vulnerable. Start today—who needs your kindness, compassion and help?

Read It: Jeremiah 22 v 1, 3

This is what the Lord *says: "Go down to the palace of the king of Judah [Jehoiakim] and proclaim this message there … : 'Do what is just and right. Rescue from the hand of the oppressor, the one who has been robbed. Do no wrong or violence to the foreigner, the fatherless or the widow, and do not shed innocent blood in this place.'"*

Discuss It

- *Would you rather…*
    a. *hide a belt under a rock and dig it up again after three years telling people their country would be destroyed?*
    b. *smash a pot in front of a country's leaders and announce their country would be ruined?*
    c. *visit the king and tell him to change his ways and look after the poor?*
- *Have you ever thought before that real worship includes really caring about others? Why is this good news and why is it challenging?*
- *Who is vulnerable or poor that needs your kindness and compassion?*
- *What could you do to help?*

Pray It

Dear God, thank you that you care for everyone but especially the poor and vulnerable. I'm sorry for the times when I don't care enough for the poor and vulnerable around me. Help me to live, speak and act justly for you today. Amen.

Do It

Why not make a donation to the food bank or volunteer to help at another local Christian charity working with people in need?

DAY 25

Memory Verse

"Call to me and I will answer you and tell you great and unsearchable things you do not know."

JEREMIAH 33 v 3

VERSE-MEMORISING TOP TIPS

Write It
Visualise It
Act It
Sing It
Record It
Use an App
... and repeat, repeat, repeat!

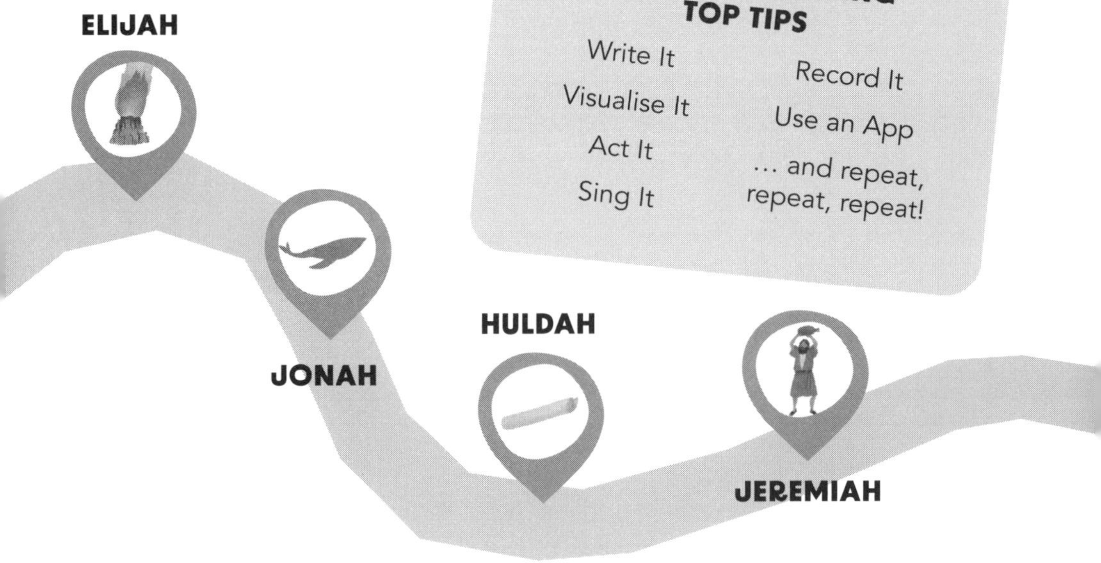

Week Six

Exile

DAY 26

Daniel: Far from Home

DANIEL 1, 6

Our Story

Have you ever eaten foreign food that is very different to what you are used to? Maybe on holiday or in a city full of different cultures? What did you eat—cactus, chicken feet, jellyfish?

God's Story

For the people in today's Bible story everything, not just the food, is foreign and strange. Remember God's messengers repeatedly warned the people to worship God and look after the poor, or Jerusalem would be destroyed and they would be taken to a foreign land, exiled. They didn't listen. So from around 600 BC some of God's people were taken from Jerusalem to Babylon, 900 miles away. Among them were some who still wanted to love and serve God…

Daniel's Story

Daniel was a young man when the Babylonians conquered Jerusalem. King Nebuchadnezzar marched Daniel and his friends to Babylon, where, chosen for their nobility, good looks, perfect physical condition and an ability to learn they were told they would be serving the king. They were renamed after Babylonian gods, trained in Babylonian courtly ways and given the Babylonian king's food and drink...

"I won't eat food forbidden by my God! Not today, not tomorrow, never," said Daniel. "Neither will we," said his friends. "We will have only vegetables and water. We trust God to keep us healthy and fit."

Healthier and fitter after ten days than all the other young men, Daniel and his friends remained true to God in diet and worship. And, after three years they amazed King Nebuchadnezzar with their wisdom and insight that surpassed all the other courtiers. Daniel was promoted to rule over the province of Babylon. And his friends were appointed alongside him.

Several kings came and went and many years passed. Daniel's exceptional leadership made other governors jealous. They watched to find fault, waiting to destroy him, but Daniel was blameless. So they conferred and connived and laid a treacherous trap. They crept to King Darius, convincing him that everyone, by law, should pray only to him for 30 days. Prayer to another would mean death by lion.

When Daniel heard this new law, he... opened his window as usual, faced his homeland Jerusalem as usual, and prayed as usual. "I will pray to my God three times today, three times tomorrow and three times every day for ever," said Daniel.

The snitches brought Daniel in. In great distress King Darius, knowing his law must stand, said, "May your God, whom you serve continually, rescue you". The stone was then rolled over the mouth of the lion's den and sealed.

Daniel was inside.

"Today, tomorrow and for ever I will trust my God," said Daniel as he turned to face his furry roommates. They were large, muscular and clearly had not had dinner. They certainly trumped him in the food chain. Their eating would be ruthless and efficient...

King Darius did not eat or sleep. Eventually when morning came he rushed back to the den and called out, "Daniel, was your God able to rescue you from the lions?"

"They have not hurt me!" came the reply.

The delighted King Darius pulled the living Daniel out and threw the tricksters and snitchers in...

Then Darius praised Daniel's God, saying, "He is a living God, and he will rule for ever. His kingdom will never be destroyed, and his power will never come to an end. He saves and rescues; he performs wonders and miracles in heaven and on earth. He saved Daniel from being killed by the lions."

God's Story

Even when they were far away from home—far from the promised land—God kept some of his people in a strong and trusting relationship with him—because the promise of all nations and all people being blessed through Abraham's family still needed to be fulfilled. Neither the power of the Babylonians nor the failure of his people could stop God from keeping his promises and working out his plan.

Our Story

Daniel and his friends refused to blend in to a culture that did not know or follow God. They lived differently to everyone else in Babylon because they trusted God. They put God first. And they did that even if it meant probable death. If we are serious about following God and living his way, we will sometimes feel different and we'll have to be different. Are you up for that challenge?

Read It: Daniel 6 v 25-28

Then King Darius wrote to all the nations and peoples of every language in all the earth:

"May you prosper greatly!
I issue a decree that in every part of my kingdom people must fear and reverence the God of Daniel.
For he is the living God
and he endures for ever;
his kingdom will not be destroyed,
his dominion will never end.
He rescues and he saves;
he performs signs and wonders
in the heavens and on the earth.
He has rescued Daniel
from the power of the lions."

So Daniel prospered during the reign of Darius and the reign of Cyrus the Persian.

Discuss It

- *Have you ever eaten foreign food that is very different to what you are used to?*
- *How did Daniel respond to the challenges and threats of living in a foreign culture?*
- *In what ways can we live differently and boldly as we choose to put God first?*
- *What truths about God can we remember that will help us to live his way when it's hard or risky?*

Pray It

Dear God, thank you that you can shut the mouths of lions and open the hearts of kings. Help me to trust you and live boldly even when it means being different. Help other people to see your way is best through the choices we make. Amen.

Do It

Grab vegetables or fruit to munch and roar out a way you can be bold for God.

DAY 27

Esther: Time to Step Up

THE BOOK OF ESTHER

Our Story

Have you ever been in a competition? Races on sports day, a bake off, a chess tournament, battle of the bands, a photography contest? Have you ever come first place or got a prize?

Did your winning change the course of history or save many lives?

God's Story

Today we're diving into the book of Esther—where God isn't mentioned once! However, he is the one working behind the scenes miraculously to save and preserve his people—and it all begins with a selfish tyrant and a beauty pageant. The king's officials travelled the land of Persia, searching every neighbourhood, community and tribe for beautiful girls. This included communities of God's exiled people. (In this part of the Bible they are called Jews.)

Esther's Story

Esther was a beautiful, Jewish orphan. She was living in Persia in exile with her cousin Mordecai when the king's men came to call. They made her enter a beauty competition. Let's call it "Miss Persia". The winner would marry the king.

After a year of pampering and preparations (oils, make-up and perfumes), Esther went to meet the king...

King Xerxes thought she was an absolute stunner, and he immediately made her his queen.

Now, about the same time as Esther became queen, Horrible Haman was made that empire's version of Prime Minister or Chief of Staff. (Boo!) (He wasn't actually called Horrible Haman, just Haman.) Horrible Haman convinced the king to make a law so that everyone had to bow to him. (Boo!) However, some people, like Mordecai and his friends, refused. They would rather die than bow down to anyone other than God! (Hooray!)

Now, Horrible Haman hated the Jews, and Mordecai especially, so he told the king about their disobedience and advised that they should be destroyed. So a law was made and a day chosen when ALL God's people would be killed. (Boo!)

Nobody knew about Esther's faith and Jewish identity because Mordecai had forbidden her from talking about it. He wanted to protect her and keep her safe. But now this had to change.

"Esther," her cousin sent a message to her. "No more secrets. Go plead with the king for your people."

"But Mordecai, if I go to the king uninvited I could die," Esther replied. (Boo!)

"But Esther," said Mordecai, "if you don't go, you will certainly die".

Esther was wise. Esther was brave. Esther asked her people to fast with her for three days. Then she acted... and...

The king was delighted to see his new wife, gorgeously dressed in her best royal robes. He welcomed her into the throneroom and accepted her invitation to a feast that night. (Hooray!) Horrible Haman was invited too.

Esther ended this first banquet with a request for both of them to dine with her again the following evening... (Hooray!)

At the second feast Esther turned to the king and asked, "Would you please save my life? And spare my people from destruction, slaughter and annihilation?"

Xerxes was horrified and enraged, and demanded to know whose evil plan this was...

"Horrible Haman," said Esther, pointing at the other dinner guest. (Boo!)

"Then he will die," said the King, "and your people will be saved". (Hooray!)

And so it was. What a turning of the tables! What a response to the prayers and fasting of God's people. What a rescue for God's people. (Hooray!)

And what a wise, brave and prayerful beauty queen.

God's Story

Esther was positioned uniquely to speak up on behalf of God's people as they faced destruction. Brave but frightened, she learned that prayer, fasting and faith in the God who is always working behind the scenes changes seemingly impossible situations. Through Esther, God's salvation plan to make his people a blessing to all people everywhere continued.

Our Story

Esther was the only Jew in the palace and at first she kept her faith hidden. Maybe you feel alone and embarrassed and so you keep your faith secret too. But God has put you in your school and neighbourhood for a reason. So be brave. Like Esther and Mordecai, you can pray and take action and be known as one of God's people.

Read It: Esther 4 v 14-16

> *[Mordecai said] "If you remain silent at this time, relief and deliverance for the Jews will arise from another place, but you and your father's family will perish. And who knows but that you have come to your royal position for such a time as this?"*
>
> *Then Esther sent this reply to Mordecai: "Go, gather together all the Jews who are in Susa, and fast for me. Do not eat or drink for three days, night or day. I and my attendants will fast as you do. When this is done, I will go to the king, even though it is against the law. And if I perish, I perish."*

Discuss It

- *Like in Esther's time, God's people are still under threat in some parts of the world. Do you have any ideas which are the three most dangerous countries to be a Christian today? (Find out the answer as part of "Do It".)*
- *In what ways might God have put you in your neighbourhood, school or workplace to serve him and help other people?*
- *What brave things might God be calling us to pray about, fast for and take action on?*

Pray It

Dear God, thank you that we are free to worship you in safety. Help us to be brave like Esther and to use our influence to serve you. Please strengthen Christians around the world in danger because of their faith. Thank you that even when we can't see it, you are working out your good plan. Amen.

Do It

Find out about Christians who are persecuted and the most difficult places to be a Christian. Pray for them. Look up the Open Doors watchlist to find out more: https://www.opendoorsuk.org/persecution/countries

DAY 28

Nehemiah: Rebuilding God's People

THE BOOK OF NEHEMIAH

Our Story

Can you remember a time when you received some terrible news about someone you really care about? Were you able to carry on as normal—or was it all you could think about?

It is never easy to hear bad news—it's even harder if the person or people who are facing the problem are far away.

God's Story

In today's story, we are still in the period of time when many of God's people are in exile in a foreign land. And a man called Nehemiah gets some bad news. His family report that their home city of Jerusalem is in crisis. It's a total mess. But God has just the man for the job, because Nehemiah happens to be an elite member of the Persian king's security force …

Nehemiah's Story

His wine was safe. I'd tested it and was serving at King Artaxerxes' table as usual when he noticed that I had lost my usual cheer. "Nehemiah, why do you look so downcast?" he asked.

Fearfully, I flung a prayer heavenwards.

"I've heard some desperate news, king. My home city is ruined. My people are in crisis…"

I flung up another prayer.

"Your Majesty, may I return to aid the rebuilding? Be granted safe passage? Take wood from your forests for reconstruction?"

And because the gracious hand of God was upon me, the king granted my requests.

After four months of travelling, we arrived home. I inspected Jerusalem's walls by night—the walls that had been built to keep the people safe. It was worse than I imagined. There was no security! I wanted to quit! But because God had put this in my heart I gathered the leaders and said, "Come, let us rebuild the walls. The God of heaven will give us success."

Neighbouring foreign tribes watched the walls grow, disturbed that someone had come to help the Israelites. They mocked us: "If a fox climbed on it, he would break down that wall!" they said. Incensed, they planned attacks, plotted to kill me, spread false rumours of my rebellion against the king and hired pretend prophets, all in an attempt to put an end to the work.

However, we persevered—because God had put this in our hearts. We grafted from dawn until the stars came out—high priests, goldsmiths, perfume-makers. Half stood guard against the threat while the rest continued on the wall nearest their homes, with spears in one hand and tools in the other.

After 52 days, the walls were completed. A cheer went up. Our enemies clearly saw that the gracious hand of God was upon us.

In celebration we gathered at the Water Gate. The priest Ezra read Moses' laws from a high platform and as the priests explained about God's love and faithfulness and about how we had sinned, the crowd's sadness swelled. "This day is for the Lord," I said. "Do not grieve, for the joy of the Lord is your strength. Pause! Feast! Feed the poor! Come back tomorrow."

For the next month we heard our history, and we worshipped, confessed, fasted and recommitted ourselves to God and each other. Then we dedicated the walls. The priests blessed and processed in different directions, with cymbals, trumpets, harps and two humongous choirs. Our rejoicing was so loud we could be heard for miles around.

If King Artaxerxes could see me now! Nehemiah, downcast? Not anymore! For Jerusalem's walls and God's people have been rebuilt.

God's Story

God's people were as run down and ruined as Jerusalem's walls. God sent Nehemiah to weep and work for change. One day, centuries later, another would come who would cry and grieve over Jerusalem. He would reveal her sin and warn of judgment. But then he would take it all on himself. Jesus has the power to totally rebuild not just our walls but our whole lives.

Our Story

Today, God's people (his church) still need building up and strengthening. God calls each of us to play our part, often close to where we live. That probably won't mean putting bricks in a wall. It will mean using what God has given us—our time, energy and things we're good at—to help and serve his people. Let's get stuck in!

Read It: Nehemiah 2 v 1-5

> *In the month of Nisan in the twentieth year of King Artaxerxes, when wine was brought for him, I took the wine and gave it to the king. I had not been sad in his presence before, so the king asked me, "Why does your face look so sad when you are not ill? This can be nothing but sadness of heart."*
>
> *I was very much afraid, but I said to the king, "May the king live forever! Why should my face not look sad when the city where my ancestors are buried lies in ruins, and its gates have been destroyed by fire?"*
>
> *The king said to me, "What is it you want?"*
>
> *Then I prayed to the God of heaven, and I answered the king, "If it pleases the king and if your servant has found favour in his sight, let him send me to the city in Judah where my ancestors are buried so that I can rebuild it."*

Discuss It

- *What brave move did Nehemiah make to be part of God's plan?*
- *What did Nehemiah's enemies do to try and stop the walls being rebuilt?*
- *How can you get stuck in where you live in order to serve God's people?*

Pray It

Dear God, thank you that we get stuck in and help to build up your people, the church. Please show us how we can do that. Give us courage and determination like Nehemiah to take risks and serve your cause in the world. Amen.

Do It

In Nehemiah it says when the walls of Jerusalem were finally rebuilt, the people's rejoicing could be heard far and wide! Play your favourite worship song really loudly and march round your house singing to God at the top of your voices.

DAY 29

Malachi: Rescuer Expected

THE BOOK OF MALACHI

Our Story

Have you ever watched the sun rise? Maybe from a tent, balcony, hill, hot air balloon or plane? Did you know that birds start singing and the sky gets lighter an hour before the sun appears? (Two hours before, if you are a robin.) It's twilight. It's dark, but when the birds start singing the promise of change is real and near. The sun is arriving. The light is coming into the world.

God's Story

In today's story we've reached the end of the Old Testament. It's a dark time for God's people. They've returned from exile, but it's not the fresh start they need and had dreamed about. Jerusalem's temple and walls are rebuilt but the people are not living in God's light. Malachi, the last Old Testament prophet, comes to challenge the people to live wholeheartedly for God. But he also promises that the "sun of righteousness" will soon rise. A new day will dawn. So, as we wrap up the Old and welcome the New, let's look back on three of God's biggest promises and look forward to their fulfilment.

Malachi's Story

Let's look *back*... God anointed David. He was a great king. He defeated Goliath, who symbolised death, and united God's people in worship. But by the end of the Old Testament, although God's people are back in their homeland they have no king. They are ruled by Persia.

Looking *forward*, God tells his people through Malachi that he will send a greater ruler to defeat not a giant but our real enemies of sin and death—Jesus, from David's family line, the anointed one, the Messiah.

Let's look *back* again… remember God rescued his people from Egypt? The key to it all was a spotless lamb, offered on behalf of the people, its blood painted on the doorposts. The lamb died so they could escape. But now, at the end of the Old Testament, God's people are bringing imperfect, diseased lambs to the temple to be sacrificed. Through Malachi, God said, "Shut the temple doors!" This isn't working. A better sacrifice is needed to bring the ultimate rescue from sin and death.

Looking *forward*, God promises his people through Malachi that a messenger will come and announce the arrival of the ruler who will fulfil God's rescue plan. Centuries later, a wild prophet called John pointed at Jesus and said, "Look! The lamb of God who takes away the sins of the world". On the cross, Jesus sacrificed his life to take our sins, end the darkness and bring us God's sunrise.

Let's look *back* for a final time… King Solomon built God a home, a temple where he lived and met with his people. God moved in and a cloud of glory followed and filled the place. But then the temple was destroyed when the people were exiled. And by the end of the Old Testament, around 450 BC, though the temple had been rebuilt, God's glory had not returned.

In our final look *forward*, God promises his people through Malachi that there will be another day when, "suddenly the Lord you are seeking will come to his temple". God would come to Jerusalem again! Centuries later, Jesus visited the temple; but more than that, Jesus *was* the temple. He is how God dwelled on earth—he is where God and his people can meet again. And still today, Jesus dwells on earth in his people by his Holy Spirit, to live with us every day.

God's Story

Through Malachi, God gives strong words of warning to the people: "I will come near you for judgment". However, these challenging words are balanced with beautiful promises of hope. Those who worship God wholeheartedly, Malachi says "will go out and leap like calves". Over them the "sun of righteousness will rise with healing in its wings". It will be a 400-year wait but Jesus, the promised ruler, the perfect sacrifice and God's presence with us, is coming!

Our Story

Our world may still feel dark, but the Son of God has now come. His light and presence can fill our hearts. In him we can experience healing and hope.

Read It: Malachi 3 v 1; 4 v 1-2

I will send my messenger, who will prepare the way before me. Then suddenly the Lord you are seeking will come to his temple; the messenger of the covenant, whom you desire, will come," says the L*ORD* *Almighty.*

"Surely the day is coming; it will burn like a furnace. All the arrogant and every evildoer will be stubble, and that day that is coming will set them on fire," says the Lord Almighty. "Not a root or a branch will be left to them. But for you who revere my name, the sun of righteousness will rise with healing in its rays. And you will go out and frolic like well-fed calves."

Discuss It

- *What was God's solution to there no longer being a king on the throne in Jerusalem and over his people?*
- *What was God's solution to a sacrificial system and priests that could not take away the people's sin?*
- *What was God's solution to his presence no longer being in the temple in Jerusalem?*
- *It must have been amazing to be a prophet like Malachi. But why is it even better to be a follower of God living now, after Jesus has lived on earth?*

Pray It

Dear God, thank you for keeping all of the hundreds of the promises you gave your people in the Old Testament Thank you that when days are dark and difficult you promise that you are with us. Thank you that as surely as the sun will rise, Jesus is risen, and he will continue to rise with healing in his wings. Amen.

Do It

Set the alarm early when the weather is clear and calm. Watch the sunrise. Listen to the birds. Thank Jesus that he has "risen with healing in his wings".

Or...

Muddle up the cards on your storyline. See if your adults (or you) can put them back in the right order—without checking out the numbers or dates on the back!

DAY 30

Memory Verse

"I know the plans I have for you ... plans to prosper you and not to harm you, plans to give you hope and a future."

JEREMIAH 29 v 11

VERSE-MEMORISING TOP TIPS

Write It

Visualise It

Act It

Sing It

Record It

Use an App

... and repeat, repeat, repeat!

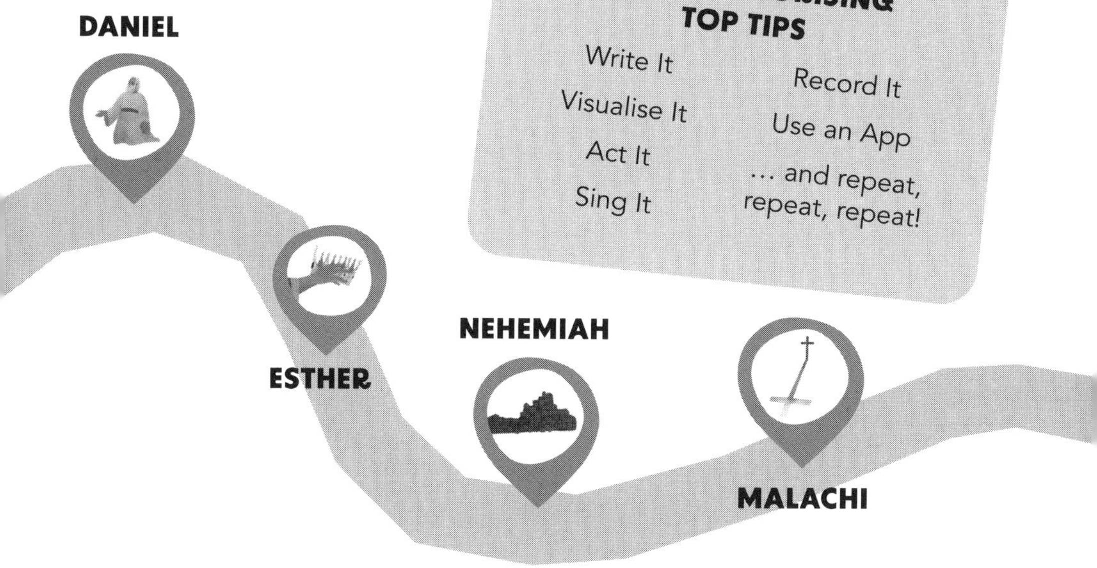

Week Seven

Jesus

DAY 31

The Birth of Jesus: God With Us

LUKE 1 v 26 – 2 v 20; MATTHEW 1 v 18 – 2 v 12

Our Story

Have you ever felt very afraid? How did you respond to the fear? Maybe you froze—you couldn't talk and your breathing went funny?

On the other hand, can you remember a time when you felt totally the opposite—you were so excited and joyful it was like you were going to pop?

God's Story

Today's story is full of terror and joy. God's people have waited and waited for the promised Rescuer and in today's story he arrives. God's messengers had given loads of details about what the Rescuer would be like. We've seen some of them in the last few sessions. One prophet, Micah, foretold that one little town would be important in God's plan. Ruth and David both lived here... any idea where this might be?

Birth Story

Mary was terrified—angels are scary! Mary was flabbergasted. Mary had to sit down... But also, Mary had to tell someone the wonderful news the angel had given her. She'd been chosen by God to have a miraculous baby. She was to call him Jesus, meaning "God saves". He would be God's Son and his kingdom would never end.

Mary rushed to see her cousin Elizabeth, who was also pregnant. Upon hearing Mary's news Elizabeth's baby jumped for joy inside her. Mary sang, "My soul praises the Lord; my spirit rejoices in God my Saviour".

So we've got one rejoicing mum, one joy-filled baby… and one terrified husband to be…

Joseph was also visited by an angel. He freaked out too—wouldn't you?! Angels are scary! The angel told him not to break up with Mary. She was going to have a baby but no human dad would be involved because God was his father. And Joseph believed what the angel had said and he married Mary.

Nine months later Mary and Joseph were in Bethlehem. (The Romans were in charge, and had made them go there to be counted.) Whilst they were there Jesus was born—in animal quarters with hay for a mattress.

It was time for God's angels to get busy again… There were shepherds out watching their sheep near Bethlehem. Suddenly an angel burst out of the night sky and terrified them. "Do not be afraid," the angel, shiny and glorious, shouted. "I've brought good news of great joy that will be for all the people: a Saviour has been born to you. Go see. He is wrapped up and lying in a trough." Countless angels then appeared, chanting God's praises and lighting up the night sky.

The shepherds ran to see their "Saviour"—and there he was, just as the angels had said, bundled up and lying in a manger! Amazed and full of joy, they told everyone about what they had seen and heard.

Meanwhile, foreign astrologers from the East did not get an angel visit. Instead, they spotted a new star. It told of a king born to the Jews. It led them to where Jesus was. Overjoyed, they bowed down, gave gifts and worshipped him too.

So we have one rejoicing mum, one joy-filled baby, countless joyous angels, joyful shepherds, overjoyed wise men and an unbreakable promise of good news, salvation and great joy for all the world.

God's Story

Hundreds of years earlier, the prophet Micah had foretold, "Bethlehem, out of you I will bring a ruler for Israel, whose family line goes back to ancient times". The promise to Abraham that ALL nations and peoples would be blessed through his family was coming true. This Rescuer, Jesus, was and still is for everyone, everywhere.

Our Story

Jesus did not come as a superhero. He was born and brought up like one of us. He experienced pain, tiredness, mud, hunger and family life. So remember, no matter how you are feeling, you can turn to Jesus. Are you afraid? Hopeless? Excited? Jesus gets it and he wants to give you his joy and be with you.

Read It: Luke 2 v 8-13

And there were shepherds living out in the fields near by, keeping watch over their flocks at night. An angel of the Lord appeared to them, and the glory of the Lord shone around them, and they were terrified. But the angel said to them, "Do not be afraid. I bring you good news that will cause great joy for all the people. Today in the town of David a Saviour has been born to you; he is the Messiah, the Lord. This will be a sign to you: you will find a baby wrapped in cloths and lying in a manger."

Suddenly a great company of the heavenly host appeared with the angel, praising God.

Discuss It

- *What is surprising about where and how Jesus was born?*
- *What does this show us about God, who he cares for and who he came for?*
- *According to the angels, why is the arrival of Jesus such good news?*
- *How is this good news for us and our world today?*

Pray It

How are you feeling today? Afraid? Full of joy? Let's tell Jesus about it:

Dear Jesus, thank you that you became a human like us and you know how we feel. Thank you that you came to rescue our world and bring us great joy. Help us to believe the good news announcement of the angels and to come to you like the shepherds. Amen.

Do It

Grab a tea towel or a pair of angel wings. Pretend to be a shepherd or angel. Go back and find the words they said and announce joyfully to anyone or anything that will listen that the Saviour of the world has been born!

DAY 32

The Baptism of Jesus: God Alongside Us

MARK 1 v 4-11; JOHN 1 v 29

Our Story

Have you ever been to a show where, before the main event, there was an opening act? The opening act prepares the crowd for the much more important main act to follow. This support act is aiming to engage the audience, warm them up, and build excitement, energy and anticipation.

God's Story

In today's story, the main act, the Rescuer, the one God's people had been waiting for, is about to go public. Jesus and his cousin John are now about 30 years old. And John is the warm-up act. He is like the wild, Old Testament prophet Elijah. He warns the people about their wrongdoing and prepares them for their Rescuer.

Baptism Story

John was a bit unusual. He was a bit more than a bit unusual—he was strange, very strange. He wore clothes made from camel hair and ate only bugs and wild honey. He lived in the desert wilderness, hollered incessantly about God and got lots of people wet.

As a baby, John had leapt in his mother's womb when he heard about the coming Saviour. At 30, his heart leapt as crowds came from around Jerusalem to hear him talk about this Saviour and how their wrongdoing could be forgiven by God. "Stop lying. Tell the truth! Stop your cruelty. Be kind! Repent—think and live differently, and God will forgive you!" he yelled. Long lines of people queued up by the Jordan River. They wanted to show in baptism that they were with God rather than running away from him.

However, not everything John said made sense. What did he mean when he said, "The kingdom of heaven is getting closer"? And who was coming who was "more powerful" and would "baptise with the Holy Spirit and with fire?"

One day the crowds watched as John refused to baptise a man... the man was about his age.

The queue nudged and muttered. "Why will John not baptise him?"

"What did John call him?"

"The Lamb of God," someone called out.

"Who takes away the sins of the world," another added.

"I need to be baptised by you, and yet you come to me?" John asked the man.

"John, you must," Jesus replied. "This is how my Father wants me to get started."

The water swirled as John plunged Jesus into the river. And as Jesus emerged it was like the heavens were torn open. God's Spirit, like a dove, rested upon him and a voice declared, "This is my Son, whom I love. With him I am well pleased."

The queue fell silent as Jesus, dripping, stepped out of the water.

John was hollering again. "I have seen and I tell you that this is the Lamb of God who takes away the sins of the world."

"Eh? What's that?" an older man in the queue asked.

"He said, 'I tell you that this is the lamb of God who will take away the sins of the world,'" replied a younger man. "Pass it down the line."

God's Story

One of Jesus' names was "Immanuel"—God with us. Imagine Jesus lining up in the queue with all the other people waiting to repent of their sins and be baptised. But he didn't need to be baptised because he'd done nothing wrong. He wanted to be baptised to show that he was one of us. Jesus is like each one of us and also so *unlike* each one of us—all at the same time.

Our Story

At his baptism, even before Jesus began work on God's big rescue plan his Father in heaven told him how much he loved him and was pleased with him. It's amazing to realise that when we follow Jesus, God becomes our Father and he sees us in the same way. No matter what we have done or not done, or achieved or not achieved, he loves us and is pleased with us.

Read It: Mark 1 v 8-11

[John said to the crowds] "I baptise you with water, but he [the one who is coming] will baptise you with the Holy Spirit."

At that time Jesus came from Nazareth in Galilee and was baptised by John in the Jordan. Just as Jesus was coming up out of the water, he saw heaven being torn open and the Spirit descending on him like a dove. And a voice came from heaven: "You are my Son, whom I love; with you I am well pleased."

Discuss It

- *John the Baptist was like a support act. Who was he preparing the way for and how?*
- *How was John different to other people around him?*
- *How was Jesus different from everyone else lining up to get baptised?*
- *What happened as Jesus came out of the water and why does that matter?*
- *John was a warm-up act for Jesus. How can we point to Jesus in the time and place in which we're living?*

Pray It

Dear God, thank you that Jesus was baptised like one of us even though he didn't need to repent or have his sins washed away. Thank you that we can become your children and know that you love us and are pleased with us. Help us to be like John, pointing others to Jesus. Amen.

Do It

Go into the garden. Catch a locust. Dip it in honey and eat it!

Or, if you can't find a locust, dip something else in honey and eat it! With your mouth full, shout out, "I'm going to point to Jesus!"

DAY 33

The Miracles of Jesus: Water to Wine

JOHN 2 v 1-11

Our Story

When you get embarrassed, your heartbeat and breathing get faster, your muscles tense, blood flows to your face and stomach causing you to blush, and you instinctively hide your face and eyes.

Have you ever been embarrassed about something and felt those things happening to you?

God's Story

Today's story is about a really embarrassing situation. It is set in an ordinary village, at an ordinary wedding. The wedding celebration, as was normal in 1st-century Judea, would last up to a week. Jesus was invited to go along with his mother and his new friends—the guys who had decided to be his disciples and follow him.

Until now Jesus had not done anything extraordinary in public. He was probably known as a kind carpenter, maybe as a wise teacher—but that was about to change.

Water to Wine Story

For the first few days of the wedding celebrations, the air had been light and filled with laughter. There had been feasting, singing, dancing and speeches, and the groom had finally kissed his bride. Gladness encircled the gathered family, neighbours and friends.

But today the groom sat with his head in his hands. The embarrassment, the humiliation, the shame! He was sure he had ordered enough wine for their week-long party. But… he'd just been told it had *run out*. The party would be ruined, the guests would be shocked, the bride's family could sue. The whole region around Cana would gossip.

Mary sidled up to Jesus and whispered, "Son, they've run out of wine". Jesus' wisdom and resourcefulness had guided her through many tricky situations—she trusted he'd help her and her friends again.

"Mother, this has nothing to do with me," Jesus firmly but kindly said. "My time has not yet come…" But before he had finished, his mother strode off towards the servants. "Do exactly what he tells you," she said with a twinkle in her eye.

(True, it wasn't time yet for his greatest work—but now could be the time for him to give a sign of why he'd come and who he was. Restoring and fixing was in his bones and spirit. This could be fun!)

"Fill those six water jars up—those huge ones they use for washing," Jesus said to the servants. They filled them to the brim. "Now take some to the head waiter," Jesus told them.

Surprised, the head waiter swirled the water around in the cup. Except, to his amazement, it wasn't water he was swirling—it was wine! He breathed in its aroma, sipped it and savoured it. He smacked his lips together and took another large gulp. His eyes lit up. He grinned. He laughed. "Wow!" he whistled. "This isn't just wine. This is the most extraordinary wine I've tasted—ever."

"Hey!" he called to the groom. "I don't understand how this happened or where this came from. Most people get out the best wine first. You've saved the best until last!"

Jesus' friends had been watching. This miracle was a sign, a revelation, for them. This was not a miraculous show of power done to impress the masses. This was the sort of glorious, extraordinary, miraculous thing only God could do. Only God could take away shame, give abundant joy, and turn sadness into feasting.

"Cheers," Jesus said, nodding in their direction.

God's Story

This miracle of turning water into wine is the first of 35 recorded miracles that Jesus did. John calls them "signs" because they each show us something about who Jesus is and what Jesus came to do. Jesus was starting a new chapter—the water was being replaced with wine. This was going to be more fun, more exciting and more powerful than anything God had done so far.

Our Story

Imagine you are Andrew, one of Jesus' new disciples. You have seen Jesus baptised, heaven open, God's voice speaking, and the dove descend. Then you have spent a few days with Jesus and attended the wedding in Cana and witnessed this miracle. Who would you think he is? Why would you be excited about being friends with him?

Read It: John 2 v 7-11

> *Jesus said to the servants, "Fill the jars with water"; so they filled them to the brim.*
>
> *Then he told them, "Now draw some out and take it to the master of the banquet."*
>
> *They did so, and the master of the banquet tasted the water that had been turned into wine. He did not realise where it had come from, though the servants who had drawn the water knew. Then he called the bridegroom aside and said, "Everyone brings out the choice wine first and then the cheaper wine after the guests have had too much to drink; but you have saved the best till now."*
>
> *What Jesus did here in Cana of Galilee was the first of the signs through which he revealed his glory; and his disciples believed in him.*

Discuss It

- *What is the best food or drink you have had at a celebration?*
- *What does this miracle show us about Jesus?*
- *If you had been one of Jesus' friends and you had seen this miracle happen how would you explain it and who would you say Jesus was?*
- *Who do you normally go to when there is a problem? How does this story encourage you to go to Jesus and talk to him about it?*
- *Have you heard about or even experienced a modern-day miracle?*

Pray It

Dear Jesus, thank you that you love celebrations and marriage. Thank you that you saved, changed and healed so many people and helped in so many difficult situations when you were on earth. Thank you that your miracles are signs showing us that you are God and that you came to bring joy and feasting. Give me faith to follow you and expect the unexpected. Amen.

Do It

Buy a cheap, medium and best-quality carton or bottle of your favourite flavoured juice. Just like the head waiter at the wedding, see if you can work out which is the best quality one with your eyes closed.

DAY 34

Jesus the Friend: Changed for Good

LUKE 19 v 1-10

Our Story

If you could have any famous person round to your house for dinner, who would you invite and why? Maybe you would ask a sports star, singer, chef, actor, comedian, YouTuber, world leader or billionaire? How would you feel if that person actually turned up, uninvited, and insisted on coming in?

God's Story

By the time today's story takes place, several years have passed since Jesus turned water into wine, and he has become famous. He is now nearing the final weeks of his life and is increasingly focused on the final part of his mission. However, that doesn't mean he doesn't care about the people he meets—including one short, lonely little man who is curious about him and needs him desperately. So, on the way, Jesus interrupts his journey to befriend, seek and save the most unlikely of people...

Zacchaeus' Story

Zacchaeus had a large house and a large wallet but a very small number of friends. He was the tax boss. He made a lot of money, because he lied, cheated and thieved. In short, he was a scumbag—and speaking of short, he was definitely that too.

One day the town of Jericho was buzzing with excitement. A famous teacher and healer was passing through. Zacchaeus wanted to see him. But pushing to the front was useless—no one would let him through. He couldn't sit on anyone's shoulders—he had no friends. And when he tried standing on tiptoes, he was still too short.

The noise and cheering got louder… What about climbing a tree? Yes! He ran ahead of the crowds. It was undignified, and not the kind of thing that rich, successful men did—but Zacchaeus didn't care! Up he clambered, scratched and out of breath, but high enough for a fantastic view. He had to see who the visitor was!

"Jesus is coming!" shrieked the children.

Zacchaeus flicked a twig from his sandal. Then everything fell silent. He looked down. Jesus looked up. "Zacchaeus!" he said. "Come down immediately. I must stay at your house today."

Zacchaeus almost fell out of the tree. Jesus knew his name! Jesus wanted to come to his house for dinner!

The crowd muttered grumpily. Why was Jesus going to the house of this sinner, this thief? Did Jesus not know who he was? What he was like?

Zacchaeus wasn't listening. He climbed down and half-jogged, half-skipped beside Jesus all the way home. This couldn't be happening to him, the little, lying, thieving, cheat, could it? Did Jesus really want to be friends with *him*?!

The nosey crowd followed, but Zacchaeus took Jesus inside and closed the door... They were clearly sitting and talking… Oh, what were they saying?

Suddenly, Zacchaeus stood up and flung the door open. "I'm sorry," he shouted. "I've been mean and nasty to all of you—but right now I give half of everything I have to the poor." The crowd gasped. "And if I've cheated anybody, I will pay them back four times as much." He rummaged in his wallet. "Simeon, I took ten extra denarii from you last tax day. Here—have forty."

"Hooray!" shouted Simeon

"Hooray!" the crowd cheered.

Jesus stood beside his new friend, beaming. "I came to seek and save lost people like Zacchaeus. And today salvation has come to this house."

God's Story

Jesus loves people—even greedy people, even friendless people, even people who get things wrong and mess things up—people like us. Jesus was nicknamed "the friend of sinners". And his mission was to "seek and save the lost" and bring salvation wherever he went.

Our Story

Now Jesus wants to be *our* friend and come into *our* lives. And as we understand how much he loves us, he'll reshape our hearts to make new positive choices and put things right. Will you welcome him gladly like Zacchaeus did? And don't worry, you won't need to climb a tree first!

Read It: Luke 19 v 5-10

> *When Jesus reached the spot, he looked up and said to him, "Zacchaeus, come down immediately. I must stay at your house today." So he came down at once and welcomed him gladly.*
>
> *All the people saw this and began to mutter, "He has gone to be the guest of a sinner."*
>
> *But Zacchaeus stood up and said to the Lord, "Look, Lord! Here and now I give half of my possessions to the poor, and if I have cheated anybody out of anything, I will pay back four times the amount."*
>
> *Jesus said to him, "Today salvation has come to this house, because this man, too, is a son of Abraham. For the Son of Man came to seek and to save the lost."*

Discuss It

- *What desperate things did Zacchaeus do to try and see who Jesus was? Why was he so determined, do you think?*
- *Zacchaeus was a bully and a cheat. Do you know someone like this? How does it feel to know that Jesus wants to be their friend too?*
- *After Zacchaeus had spent just a little bit of time with Jesus, what radical choices did he make?*
- *What positive changes is Jesus inspiring you to make? Are there ways that you could put things right and make a new start?*

Pray It

Dear Jesus, thank you that you are the best friend we will ever have. Thank you that you're not put off by what we've done or what we look like. Thank you that you came to save people like us, because you love people like us. Please help us to put things right and become more like you. Amen.

Do It

Go and climb a tree or find a high place, and once you are there, thank Jesus for being the best friend you will ever have.

DAY 35

Memory Verse

"A Saviour has been born to you; he is Christ the Lord."

LUKE 2 v 11

VERSE-MEMORISING TOP TIPS

Write It

Visualise It

Act It

Sing It

Record It

Use an App

... and repeat, repeat, repeat!

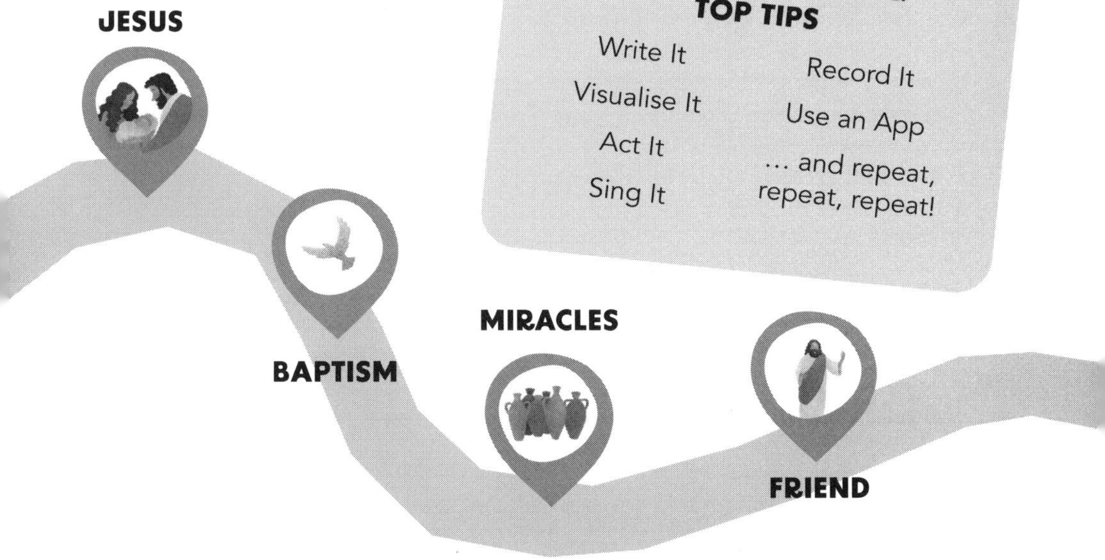

Week Eight

Easter

DAY 36

Jesus the King: A Noisy Welcome

LUKE 19 v 28-40

Our Story

What's the biggest crowd you have ever been in? Maybe you were at a music concert or sports match? Maybe you were in a crowd at a fireworks display, in an airport, zoo, museum or theme park? Most crowds gather when there is something important to see, celebrate or do....

God's Story

Hundreds of years before today's story, the prophet Zechariah had foretold that God's rescuing King would enter Jerusalem in a victory parade on a donkey.

And going even further back in the story of God's people, do you remember the escape from Egypt—the Passover? John must have been thinking of that event when he called Jesus "the Lamb of God" at Jesus' baptism. And it's no coincidence that Jesus is arriving in Jerusalem just as people are preparing for Passover...

Jesus the King Story

The roads to Jerusalem were busy and full
The pilgrims were feeling the festival pull
They'd come in their thousands from far and near
They entered the city with joy and a cheer.

The Passover feast was the best, the tops!
When the people remembered—they never forgot—
How God had saved them through the blood of a lamb
Death passed over, a new chapter began

They'd escaped from Egypt through the Red Sea
They'd entered the promised land—eventually.

Jesus and friends went to Jerusalem too
And along the way he told two of his crew
To ask at a house about using their donkey
(He needed something humble—not grand or mighty.)

Putting cloaks as a saddle, off they went
And as they neared the city it became quite an event
The crowd began shouting and dancing and singing
The branches from palms they were waving and swinging
They took off their coats and laid them down
If they could have, they would have made Jesus a crown.

They knew him.
They'd listened.
They'd watched all his ways,
Nothing could hold back their worship and praise.

"He healed me!"
"He taught me!"
"He resurrected my brother!"
"He delivered my sister!"
"He fed my dear mother!"

"Hosanna!" they cried: "This new King will save us!
"He's the Rescuer, Saviour, the one like King David!
"He comes in peace, he comes in love.
"He's surely been sent from God above!"

"Hang on a moment!" some angry ones muttered
"This isn't quite right, there must be another.
"He's not on a war-horse and where is his sword?
"Humility? Justice? We need a warlord!"

The Pharisees too were all hot and bothered.
"Stop their praise, Jesus!" some of them hollered.

(The Pharisees, see, loved religion and rules
They made the laws and ran the schools
Jesus made them hopping mad
They thought him evil, someone bad
He wasn't their King, or the Saviour God promised
The crowds were wrong and Jesus dishonest.)

"I won't," said Jesus, "stop them saying such things—
"If they didn't say them, these rocks would sing."

God's Story

A few days after Jesus was celebrated as the victorious King, he did something shocking. While he celebrated Passover he told his friends that he was like the lamb—that he was going to be sacrificed to set people free. His body would be broken and his blood shed to bring rescue from sin and death.

Our Story

Many welcomed Jesus, but some rejected him because he was not what they expected. He wasn't doing what they thought he should do. Still today people reject Jesus because they don't agree with what he says and because he doesn't do everything they want. How about you?

Read It: Luke 19 v 36-40

> *As [Jesus] he went along, people spread their cloaks on the road. When he came near the place where the road goes down the Mount of Olives, the whole crowd of disciples began joyfully to praise God in loud voices for all the miracles they had seen:*
>
> *"Blessed is the king who comes in the name of the Lord!"*
>
> *"Peace in heaven and glory in the highest!"*
>
> *Some of the Pharisees in the crowd said to Jesus, "Teacher, rebuke your disciples!"*
>
> *"I tell you,' he replied, "if they keep quiet, the stones will cry out."*

Discuss It

- *How did the crowd celebrate the arrival of Jesus? Who did the crowd declare Jesus to be?*
- *Why is it great news that Jesus is the promised King and the sacrificed Lamb?*
- *In what ways can we welcome Jesus and celebrate him like the crowds did?*
- *What are some of the reasons why people reject Jesus today?*

Pray It

Dear God, thank you that Jesus is the true King who is also the promised Rescuer. Thank you that Jesus came not to conquer through violence but to win our hearts through love. Even if others reject Jesus, help us to welcome and celebrate him as our King. Amen.

Do It

Get out some pots and pans. Make a joyful racket and shout, "Jesus is our King!"

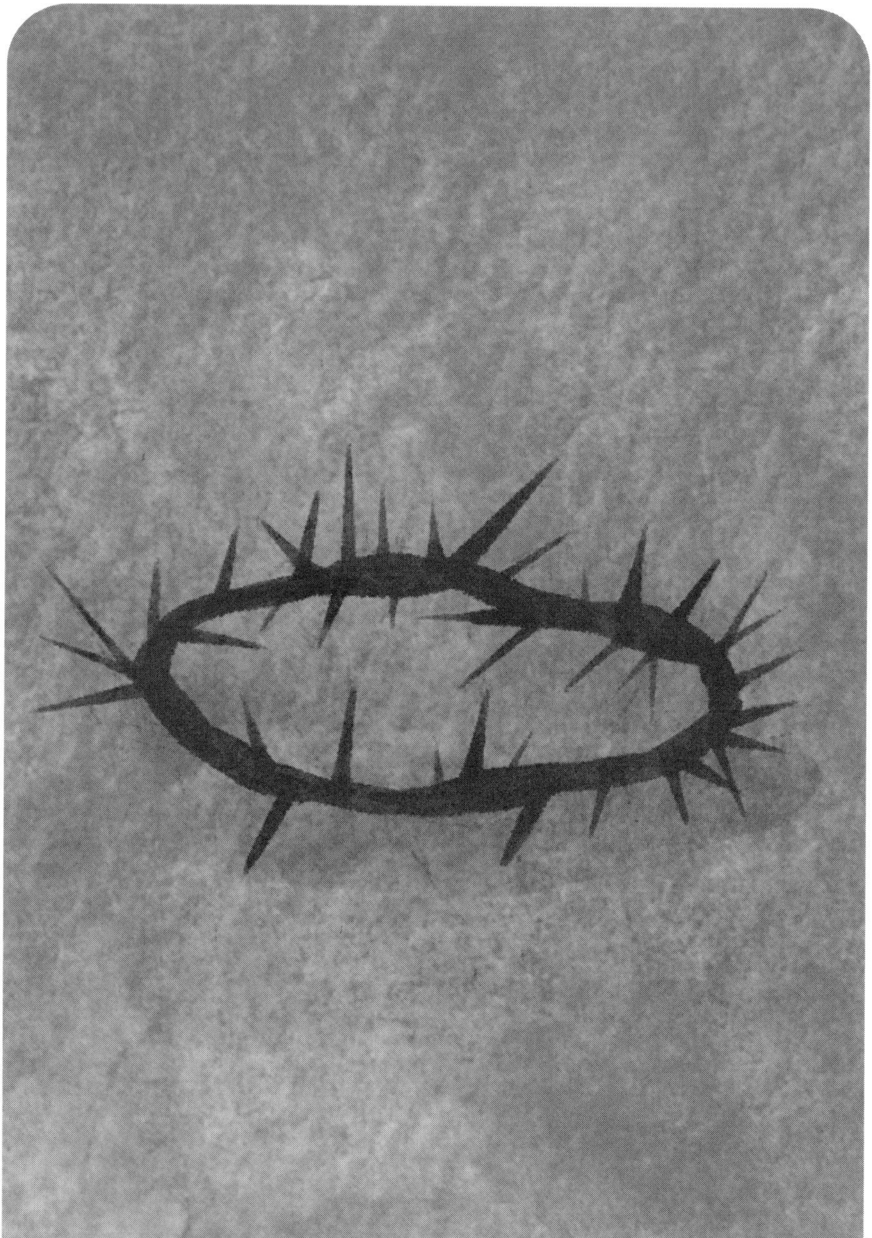

DAY 37

Jesus Is Crucified: A Loving Death

MARK 14 v 32 – 15 v 39

Our Story

The cross is the symbol of Christianity. Look around you—people wear crosses as jewellery, have cross-shaped tattoos or have cross-shaped decorations around their homes. If you flew like a bird over a very old church you would see that they are designed in the shape of a cross.

When you think about it, this is strange, because the cross was used by the Romans as the most brutal form of punishment and execution.

God's Story

A week after Jesus rode into Jerusalem on a donkey, the crowds turned against him. They wanted Jesus to overthrow the Romans, not rescue them from their sin. Jesus knows it is time for God's rescue mission, promised since Eden, to be completed. It's time to deal with our separation from God and defeat the evil snake once and for all. In today's story Jesus will be the ultimate Passover lamb who takes away the sins of the world—and he will do it by dying on a cross.

Jesus is Crucified Story

It was Thursday night. It was dark and quiet in the olive grove. Jesus was praying. Distress and sorrow shrouded his face. Sweat, like blood, fell to the ground...

The temple security forces and leaders arrived with Jesus' friend Judas. Their sly plot, to arrest and kill Jesus, was in motion. Their swords were ready, but unnecessary. Jesus stepped forward willingly. This was their hour, when darkness reigned.

At the high priest's house, Jesus' enemies tried to trap him with words. Finally, Jesus was asked, "Are you the Christ, the Son of God?" His truthfulness maddened them. "I am," he said. "He's worthy of death!" they shouted.

Very early in the morning, having been blindfolded, spat on, beaten up and bound, Jesus was taken to the Roman governor. Pilate listened to the twisted charges and Jesus' silence. He knew Jesus was innocent, but he could not convince the crowd to set Jesus free.

"Take him away!" and "Crucify him!" they demanded, louder and louder.

So Pilate gave in. He handed Jesus over. The Roman soldiers whipped him, stripped him and dressed him like royalty with a purple robe, a crown of thorns and a staff. They knelt in mocking worship. "Hail, king of the Jews," they taunted. They struck his head again and again. This was their hour, when darkness reigned.

Bruised, broken and bleeding, Jesus stumbled out of Jerusalem, carrying a cross.

At 9 o'clock, soldiers stretched Jesus out and nailed him down. A sign (for fun) hung over his head: "King of the Jews". The religious leaders sneered. The crowd jeered. Soldiers gambled for his clothes. And Jesus said, "Father, forgive them".

At 12 o'clock, a hellish darkness fell. Shame, suffering and God's judgment for sin was poured onto Jesus. Alone and in excruciating pain, Jesus cried out, "My God, why have you left me?"

At 3 o'clock Jesus shouted a final battle cry: "It is finished!" And then he died.

It seemed like evil had won, that darkness was reigning.

Yet, in that moment everything was changing. An earthquake split rocks open. Holy people rose from their graves. The temple curtain that separated people from God's presence tore from top to bottom. And a Roman centurion, who had witnessed Jesus' death, declared in awe, "Surely this man was the Son of God!"

It didn't look like it, but this actually was God's hour, when God's love reigned.

God's King had won.

God's Story

From the first human sin in Eden, God had promised a Rescuer and saviour—someone who would bring us back into relationship with him. God then gave hundreds more promises about how this would happen. At least 300 were fulfilled in Jesus' life and an amazing 28 in his death (which he had no control over). His perfect, sinless life and sacrificial death took away the sin of the world, defeated sickness and death and crushed the evil snake's power. It brought us peace with God.

Our Story

It's difficult and emotional to read about Jesus' trial and crucifixion. It's even more challenging when we understand that Jesus died for the wrong things you and I have done. We all have a choice how we respond to his sacrifice—will we be like the crowd who jeered and sneered or like the Roman centurion who watched amazed and declared, "This is the Son of God"?

Read It: Mark 15 v 33-34, 37-39

> *At noon, darkness came over the whole land until three in the afternoon. And at three in the afternoon Jesus cried out in a loud voice, "Eloi, Eloi, lema sabachthani?" (which means "My God, my God, why have you forsaken me?") ...*
>
> *With a loud cry, Jesus breathed his last.*
>
> *The curtain of the temple was torn in two from top to bottom. And when the centurion, who stood there in front of Jesus, saw how he died, he said, "Surely this man was the Son of God!"*

Discuss It

- *What strange things happened as Jesus died?*
- *What might these strange things show us about why Jesus died?*
- *How does it make you feel that Jesus died for you in this way?*
- *When you read about Jesus' death, are you more like the leaders who laughed at him or the Roman soldier who worshipped him?*

Pray It

Dear Jesus, thank you for loving us so much that you took the judgment and punishment that our sin deserves when you died on the cross. Sorry that we don't always live as if you are the King. Thank you for the power of your love that makes it possible to be your friend. Help us to share this great love with others. Amen.

Do It

Make a cross out of card or something else. Hang it somewhere to remind you that Jesus loves you.

DAY 38

Jesus Is Risen: A Great Victory

LUKE 24 v 1-12

Our Story

What is the best surprise you have ever had? A birthday party you had no idea was happening? Test results that you weren't expecting? A victory that you had not anticipated? A visit from someone that totally shocked you?

God's Story

Things are looking grim at the start of today's story. Jesus is dead. (The soldiers made sure of that by running a sword through his side.) Jesus is buried. (Joseph of Arimathea, a secret follower of Jesus', made sure of that by wrapping his corpse and laying it in his tomb.) However, some humongous surprises await Jesus' friends, because Jesus is going to keep his promises—promises that his friends have forgotten...

Jesus Is Risen Story

Jesus' friend Mary carried a heavy load of grief and her jar of spices as she walked with her friends. It was early. Dawn struggled to banish the night. It felt like the darkness would last for ever. Jesus was dead. Joanna sobbed. Both Marys caught her sorrow as they approached the tomb.

How would they sweeten and prepare their Lord's body? Pilate had granted the religious leaders their request for his toughest armed guards and a seal to protect the tomb (as if the mighty stone rolled over the entrance was not enough). Certainly, no one was getting in and no one was getting out.

But... what was that?

They stumbled. The ground shook. A tremor. A roar. A rumble… another earthquake?

And what was that?

Dazzling brightness, like lightning, white as snow. An angel! Mary was shaking in terror. She covered her eyes. She must be seeing things. The angel alighted, rolled the stone away (as if it were a flatbread) and sat down on it.

The guards, so overwhelmed by fear, had become like dead men.

The angel swung his legs, whistled and beckoned to them. "Come see the place where he lay," he said. "Where he *lay*?" Mary wondered. This was crazy. The sorrow, shock and shine were scrambling her mind.

The women cautiously entered the tomb. There was nobody there! There was NO BODY there!!! Just folded linens and a sense of something other than despair… "He's not here," the angel beamed. "He is alive! Remember what he said to you: he would be crucified, and three days later he would come back to life."

The sun broke over the horizon. A new day. Night was over.

"Go tell his friends that he is alive," laughed the angel.

Filled with joy and hope, the women returned to the others.

"This is crazy!" Peter said. "You are crazy!"

"This is nonsense!" said John. "It makes no sense!"

Even so, they raced to the tomb to see… and it was just as the women had said.

God's Story

Later, Jesus appeared to other disciples and showed them his scarred hands and feet. He ate fish to prove he was alive. Over the next 40 days, he appeared to individuals, couples and crowds—more than 500 in all.

Jesus could not have stayed dead. Sin, death and the devil had no power over him. By dying and coming back to life, he had shaken the old order of things to the core, and proved he is the serpent-crusher, the blessing-bringer, the promised King, the one all the prophets were talking about—and that he always keeps his promises.

Our Story

Jesus has gone before us and has promised that he is preparing a place for us with him after we die. Many people have questions and fears about dying. But if you are Jesus' friend, you don't need to fear death. Because Jesus is risen, one day you'll get to enjoy life with God for ever. And in the meantime, always remember—Jesus is alive.

Read It: Luke 24 v 1-7

On the first day of the week, very early in the morning, the women took the spices they had prepared and went to the tomb. They found the stone rolled away from the tomb, but when they entered, they did not find the body of the Lord Jesus. While they were wondering about this, suddenly two men in clothes that gleamed like lightning stood beside them. In their fright the women bowed down with their faces to the ground, but the men said to them, "Why do you look for the living among the dead? He is not here; he has risen! Remember how he told you, while he was still with you in Galilee: 'The Son of Man must be delivered over to the hands of sinners, be crucified and on the third day be raised again.'"

Discuss It

- *Why do you think the religious leaders wanted the tomb where Jesus was buried to be guarded?*
- *Three days later when the women visited the tomb, what emotions do you think they felt when they discovered Jesus was not there?*
- *What great problems has Jesus defeated by dying and coming back to life?*
- *These are some of the disciples Jesus actually appeared to. Who do you identify with the most?*
    - *Mary, who was full of joy when she saw Jesus was alive*
    - *The two friends on the road to Emmaus, who needed an explanation from the Bible*
    - *The disciples hiding in fear, who needed to know Jesus was with them*
    - *Thomas, who doubted it could be true until he saw Jesus for himself*
    - *Peter, who needed forgiveness for denying Jesus and failing him*

Pray It

Before we "pray it", take a moment to be quiet and ask Jesus to take away any fear of death you may have and draw close as a friend.

Dear Jesus, thank you for taking on our problem of death and defeating it. Thank you that I don't need to fear dying because you have given me eternal life. Help me to live as your friend and share this good news with others. Amen.

Do It

Set a timer for three minutes (Jesus was dead for three days). Lie down. Shut your eyes. No giggling. When the timer goes off, jump up and shout, "Jesus is alive!" As you lie there, think about Jesus' victory over death.

DAY 39

Jesus Ascended: Goodbye for Now

MATTHEW 28 v 18-20; ACTS 1 v 6-11

Our Story

Have you ever had to say goodbye to someone when you knew you wouldn't see them again for a very long time? Not the kind of goodbye you say at the end of the school day but the kind of goodbye you say when someone moves to another country. Saying that kind of goodbye can be very difficult.

God's Story

Jesus' followers thought they had said a final goodbye to him on the cross. However, for 40 days after his resurrection he appeared to them and talked about his kingdom. But then came another goodbye. In today's story we will hear about this last goodbye and how Jesus wrapped up his time on earth.

Jesus Goes Home Story

Up they went to Bethany on the Mount of Olives. This was where special things had happened—where Jesus had brought Lazarus back to life, where his friend Mary had anointed him to show her love for him, where the palm parade had begun. These things were remembered and talked about.

As they walked, Jesus' closest eleven friends started up a conversation about God's kingdom. "When will you kick out the Romans and start ruling over Israel?" they wondered. Jesus explained again that God's kingdom wasn't political or geographical. It was a spiritual kingdom, where God was King in people's hearts not in a palace.

"Hurry up!" Jesus shouted as they gathered on the hilltop. "Hush up!" he cried and raised up his voice so they could all hear: "Go and make disciples of all nations, baptise people and teach them to obey everything I have told you". He reached up his hands, blessing them, and continued, "I am with you always, to the very end of the age".

After he spoke, a special, shiny cloud began to appear. And then his body was up in the air! Jesus was rising up into a holy cloud!

Eleven chins and noses tilted up.

Eleven pairs of eyes gazed up, transfixed...

There must be a mix-up or a mess-up?

This didn't add up.

What was Jesus up to?

Then two men, dazzling and white, were standing amongst them.

(Honestly, you couldn't make this up.)

"Why are you looking up?" one said.

"Update: Jesus will return," the other said.

"Cheer up: he promised to be with you."

"Heads up: the Holy Spirit, the helper, will come to you soon."

"Will you take Jesus up on the mission he gave you?"

"So many don't know about Jesus, his love and death and resurrection."

"So be up and about kingdom business."

"Go everywhere!"

"Go to everyone!"

"Go for it!"

Now the disciples weren't upset. They were upbeat. They wouldn't give up. They would keep up Jesus' work. They lifted up their voices in worship and returned to Jerusalem.

Jesus was upon his throne, at home with his Father, in heaven.

But he had promised he would return!

He had promised them he would always be with them!

And he had promised to send his Spirit as their helper!

God's Story

A disciple follows an expert. They learn from them. Jesus' friends had been with him for three years. They had seen Jesus heal, pray, teach and love people. Now it was their turn. Jesus returned to be with his Father. He knew that if all his disciples got busy doing the kind of work he had been doing, many more people would come to know him. It was time for a whole new chapter in God's story.

Our Story

Jesus' challenge to his friends, to go and make disciples, still applies to us today. So many people still don't know about Jesus, his love and death and resurrection for them. Are you up for this challenge? Will you take Jesus up on this mission?

Read It: Acts 1 v 8-9

> *[Jesus said} "You will receive power when the Holy Spirit comes on you; and you will be my witnesses in Jerusalem, and in all Judea and Samaria, and to the ends of the earth." After he said this, he was taken up before their very eyes, and a cloud hid him from their sight.*

Discuss It

- *Have you ever made an interesting exit from somewhere?*
- *Why was it a good idea that Jesus' friends didn't stay on the Mount of Olives looking up into the sky?*
- *What mission did Jesus give his friends? In what way is this exciting, and in what way is this terrifying?*
- *Do you think they were ready for the mission they had been given? Are we?*

Pray It

Dear Jesus, thank you that you are now King in heaven. Thank you that you trained and trusted your friends to continue God's kingdom work that you began. Help us to believe that you can use us to tell people about you too. Amen.

Do It

Aim to watch the clouds (or just the sky if there are no clouds) as many times as you can today. As you watch, say to yourself, "Jesus is coming back".

(This is the most fun if you lie on your back and look for shapes in the clouds at the same time.)

DAY 40

Memory Verse

"God so loved the world that he gave his one and only Son, that whoever believes in him shall not perish but have eternal life."

JOHN 3 v 16

VERSE-MEMORISING TOP TIPS

Write It
Visualise It
Act It
Sing It
Record It
Use an App
... and repeat, repeat, repeat!

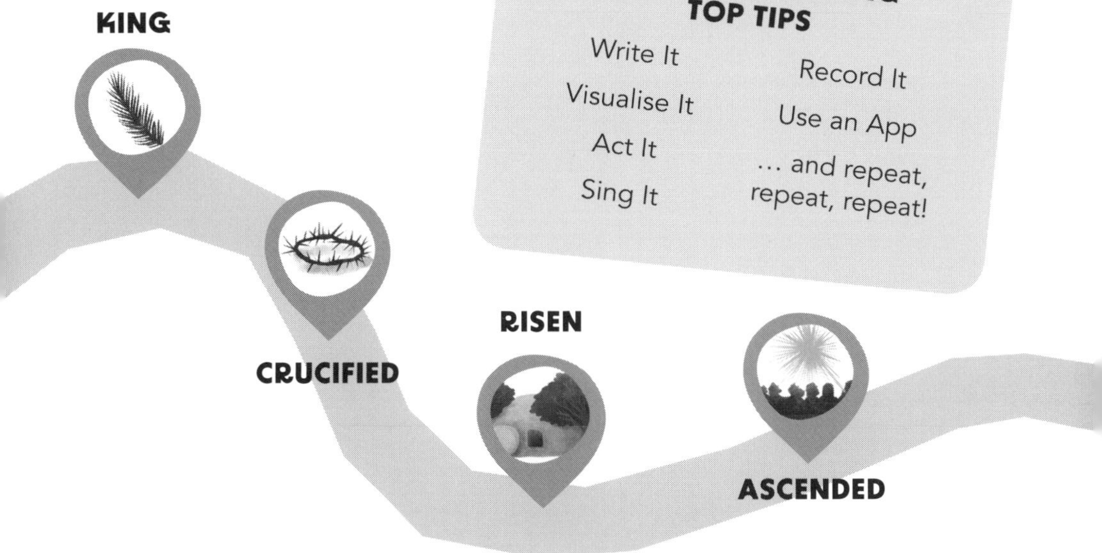

Week Nine

Mission

DAY 41

Pentecost: The Church Is Born

ACTS 2

Our Story

What qualities do your best friends have? Maybe you like friends who are strong, playful, creative and full of joy; or maybe you choose friends who are kind, gentle, encouraging and trustworthy; or maybe your friends teach you and help you understand things. Or maybe they're a mixture!

God's Story

In today's story, Jesus sends an extraordinary friend and helper to be with his followers. This story of Pentecost happens after Jesus came back to life and returned to heaven. He had promised his followers that he would not leave them alone. However, the new friend he sent maybe didn't show up in quite the way they were expecting…

Pentecost Story

Jesus' followers were expectant: waiting and wondering. When would the friend and helper arrive? Would it be obvious? Would they have to wait much longer?

They'd all gathered together in a house in Jerusalem. Like at Passover, thousands of pilgrims from many nations were there for Pentecost. They were celebrating the harvest and remembering the giving of the commandments.

Suddenly, the waiting was over! There was a wind from heaven… whirling, whipping, wild, wonderful wind, rattling and rushing through every room of the house they were staying in.

Then they saw tongues of fire… fascinating, flickering, configuring into flames that came to rest on each of their heads. It was a fire that didn't destroy. A fire that fanned their faith, filling them with the Holy Spirit, flooding them with God's presence, gifts and power.

The waiting was over. The friend and helper that Jesus had promised and the prophets had foretold had arrived.

There were loud shouts of praise to God. Their fear was gone. And they suddenly realised that each of them could speak in new languages that they had not learned to speak in.

Large crowds gathered, fascinated by these local people who could now speak to each of them in their own language. Most were utterly amazed, but some laughed.

"Are they drunk?"

"They've had too much wine."

"Be logical," Jesus' friend Peter replied. "It's only nine in the morning!"

"But what does this all mean?" the crowd asked, amazed.

Peter stood up and with new Spirit-given courage he explained...

"These men are not drunk. They are full of God's Spirit—the Spirit God promised to pour out on all people once his Rescuer Jesus had come. You put him to death by nailing him to a cross but it was impossible for death to keep hold of him. God raised him back to life. It's a fact. We've seen him. He is Lord and Christ!"

The crowds listening knew deep in their hearts that what Peter was saying was true. "What must we do?" they asked.

"Turn to God and be baptised so that your sins may be forgiven," Peter told them. "And you will receive the gift of the Holy Spirit."

And then... What a response. What understanding. What unity. And what queues, as 3,000 people who had just decided to put their faith in Jesus as their King and Saviour waited to be baptised. On this Pentecost the church was born and the Holy Spirit, as promised, was poured out on all God's people.

God's Story

At Pentecost we see the opposite of what happened at the tower of Babel. Rather than people being separated from each other, thousands were drawn together and to God. It was the birthday of the Christian church. A new chapter in God's story had begun. As the rest of the book of Acts shows, God's Spirit was no longer going to live only in a few of God's people, but in all of them.

Our Story

Peter told the crowd to "repent". This means to turn away from the things that are wrong and to go God's way. Is this something you have ever done? Maybe today is the day to ask Jesus to be your Saviour, friend and King!

And when you do, God's Holy Spirit will come and live inside you as he does with everyone who believes in Jesus. And he's not just a one-off visitor. He's our companion, our helper, our encourager and our guide. He gives us courage to talk about Jesus and do the kinds of things that Jesus did. What a gift!

Read It: Acts 2 v 1-4, 38-39

> *When the day of Pentecost came, they were all together in one place. Suddenly a sound like the blowing of a violent wind came from heaven and filled the whole house where they were sitting. They saw what seemed to be tongues of fire that separated and came to rest on each of them. All of them were filled with the Holy Spirit and began to speak in other tongues as the Spirit enabled them. ...*
>
> *Peter [said], "Repent and be baptised, every one of you, in the name of Jesus Christ for the forgiveness of your sins. And you will receive the gift of the Holy Spirit. The promise is for you and your children and for all who are far off—for all whom the Lord our God will call."*

Discuss It

- *What changes happened to Jesus' friends at Pentecost when they were filled with the Holy Spirit?*
- *What two amazing gifts did Peter promise to those who turned to Jesus?*
- *How many people became friends and followers of Jesus at Pentecost?*
- *Have you ever asked God for forgiveness and then invited the Holy Spirit to come and live inside you? Today is a day when you could do this.*
- *How do you feel about welcoming the Holy Spirit's presence into your heart? What difference would you like the Holy Spirit to make?*

Pray It

Dear God, help me to think about repenting and asking for forgiveness for the first time. And if I am a follower of Jesus then help me, Holy Spirit, to rely on you to guide me and to help me share the good news about Jesus boldly. Thank you that we can be part of your amazing worldwide church family. Amen.

Do It

On the day of Pentecost, 3,000 more people followed Jesus. Find out how many Christians there are in the world today. You'll be amazed—write the number out in full with all the zeros! You could ask Alexa, Siri, Google or Wikipedia.

DAY 42

Paul: Seeing the Light

ACTS 9

Our Story

Have you ever completely changed your mind about something? Maybe you changed the team you supported? Or when it comes to food, maybe you have converted from really not liking a food to actually enjoying it now? Or perhaps you've observed the process of conversion of a caterpillar becoming a butterfly or a tadpole becoming a frog?

God's Story

Today's story is all about a conversion and a transformation. When Peter preached at Pentecost, thousands of people changed their minds about Jesus and started to follow him as their King and Rescuer. But as more people became Jesus-followers, some powerful Jewish leaders became angry. One of them was determined to end the new Jesus movement. In today's story he has an amazing supernatural experience which leads him to totally change his mind, his life and his mission...

Saul's Story

Saul was powerful and wealthy. Saul was a Roman citizen and a Pharisee. Saul had made it his mission to destroy the newly formed Christian church.

In Jerusalem Saul had been a menace. He did everything possible to harm and persecute Jesus' followers: beating them up, dragging them off to prison, pressuring them to give up their faith and even killing them.

Saul was fixated on destroying all of Jesus' followers, everywhere. So he sped up as he approached the city of Damascus, where he knew people had started following Jesus. He must ruin them all...

Suddenly, a light from heaven flashed around him. The brilliance, brighter than the sun, blinded him. He fell to the ground, speechless.

And a voice called... "Saul, Saul, why do you persecute me?"

Instinctively, Saul knew it was God. "Who are you, Lord?" he asked. The reply was personal and specific and shocking: "I am Jesus, who you are persecuting..."

Inside Damascus three days later, the same voice called to Ananias too. (Ananias was just the sort of Jesus follower who Saul was planning to target.)

"Ananias."

"Yes, Lord?"

"Go to Saul, who is staying on Straight Street. He has been blinded, and you must go to him and pray for his healing."

"But Lord, I've heard stories about what Saul has done, and the murderous threats he has made against your people."

"Go, Ananias! I have chosen Saul to travel far and wide telling people all about me. He will even talk to great kings about who I am and what I have done."

Obediently and courageously, Ananias went. And as he prayed over Saul, something like fish scales fell from Saul's eyes. Not only could Saul see again, he had totally changed his mind about Jesus and been filled with the Holy Spirit. He could now see that Jesus was God's Son and that he needed his forgiveness. He got up, was baptised and had something to eat and drink for the first time in three days. And at once he began to preach in the synagogues, baffling the Jews by teaching and arguing that Jesus—the Jesus he had been fighting against—is God's Son.

Before long, the Jewish leaders in Damascus began plotting to kill Saul. They hated him. They hated his transformation from an enemy to a friend of Jesus. And they hated his new mission to tell everyone about the love and forgiveness Jesus could give them. But just as Saul had not been able to stop the church, Saul's new opponents could not stop him...

God's Story

When Jesus interrupted Saul (also known as Paul) on his deadly mission to destroy Christians, he also transformed him. Strangely, it was only when Saul lost his sight that he saw clearly who Jesus was. God told him, "I am sending you to the Gentiles to open their eyes and turn them from darkness to light". (A Gentile was anyone who was not an Israelite or Jew). Within days, God started to use Saul and by the end of his life he had brought the message about Jesus to people near and far, across the whole Roman world. And, as promised, he did get to speak to numerous powerful kings and rulers about Jesus.

Our Story

We sometimes think there is no way our friends would become followers of Jesus. But Saul was the least likely person to become a Jesus follower—yet he did! And not only that—he became the greatest missionary, evangelist and leader ever! So let's pray for our friends, because no one is too bad or too far from Jesus to be loved and transformed by him.

Read It: Acts 9 v 1-5

> *Saul was still breathing out murderous threats against the Lord's disciples. He went to the high priest and asked him for letters to the synagogues in Damascus, so that if he found any there who belonged to the Way, whether men or women, he might take them as prisoners to Jerusalem. As he neared Damascus on his journey, suddenly a light from heaven flashed around him. He fell to the ground and heard a voice say to him, "Saul, Saul, why do you persecute me?"*
>
> *"Who are you, Lord?" Saul asked.*
>
> *"I am Jesus, whom you are persecuting," he replied.*

Discuss It

- *On the road to Damascus, what did Saul (who was also known as Paul) completely change his mind about? Why?*
- *Why is it a big surprise that Saul spent the rest of his life travelling and telling everyone he met about Jesus?*
- *How does the change in Saul inspire us not to write off anyone from becoming a Jesus-follower?*
- *What difference is this going to make to how you pray and speak this week?*

Pray It

Dear God, thank you for meeting with Saul and transforming and then using him. Thank you that no one is out of the reach of your love. I pray that you would help my friends [say their names] come to know Jesus. Help me not to write anyone off but to believe that you can change anyone into one of your followers. Amen.

Do It

Ask an older friend or someone in your family if they can tell you a story about someone who totally changed their mind about Jesus.

DAY 43

Lydia: Good News Spreads

ACTS 16

Our Story

Imagine God sends you to a distant city to tell people all about Jesus. What would you do first? Rent a building? Offer free breakfasts? Set up a stage in the middle of the city and preach? Go door-to-door with Bibles? Invite a Christian rock band to do a week of gigs?

God's Story

Paul faced incredible challenges as he visited city after city sharing the good news of Jesus. He travelled 10,000 miles and established at least ten churches. He was whipped, shipwrecked twice, and imprisoned for nearly five years in total. In today's story, Paul and his friends are in Philippi, an important city that is now in modern-day Greece. They are hoping to begin a church there. As we'll see, the first members of this church were an interesting bunch!

Lydia's Story

I'm Lydia, and I'm part of the church family in Philippi. We are so different; there's me, a successful, single businesswoman; there's a former demon-possessed slave girl, and there's a burly Roman soldier-turned-jailer and his family. We make up Philippi's new church and we meet in my home.

It began one Sabbath when, as usual, some of us women gathered outside the city by the river to pray and talk about the ancient story of Israel and their God. (I'm not a Jew myself, but their story fascinates me.) This Sabbath we were joined by four strangers. Their leader, Paul, though small and odd-looking, was spellbinding as he shared new teaching with us about the long-awaited Messiah—Jesus, who came, died and rose again. God gently, quietly opened my heart to respond to this message. I knew it was true. Jesus was the one I was searching for. I had to hear more and persuaded Paul and his friends to stay at my house. (My business in purple cloth was booming. There was room for everyone.) My household also heard their message about Jesus and we were all baptised.

Paul and his friends continued to talk about Jesus wherever they could.

Every day they passed by a nameless slave girl. She was bound physically by her greedy owners and she was trapped on the inside by an evil spirit who would shout out of her, "These men are servants of the Most High God. They are telling you the way to be saved."

Paul became increasingly upset by her situation until he commanded the spirit, in the name of Jesus, to leave. It did! Her owners threw her out, of course, as she could no longer make money for them. She was free but friendless, so I scooped her up… But then her ex-owners started a riot and they took Paul away.

He was stripped, severely beaten and imprisoned. The others in the jail were amazed at his ability to worship and pray. Their amazement grew when at midnight, a violent earthquake shook the building. The doors flew open and the prisoners' chains fell off. In awe because no prisoners had fled, the jailer took Paul to his house, washed his wounds and peppered him with questions about what he must do to be saved. "Believe in the Lord Jesus, and you will be saved," Paul told him. So he did! His household listened too. They would no longer worship fake Roman gods. Now they would follow the one true God, Jesus. They were filled with joy and were baptised.

Like I said, we are so different. Me, the slave girl, the jailer, and more. We are Philippi's new house church.

God's Story

When Paul and his team arrived in Philippi they talked about Jesus, worshipped, prayed and talked about Jesus some more. They did this wherever they went, whoever they met, and whatever was going on. And the most unlikely people were the first to respond. The promise to Abraham that through his family all nations would be blessed was coming true. This story shows us that Jesus is for everyone and that being part of the church unites everyone.

Our Story

Paul and his friends were prepared to go anywhere and do anything so that more people could hear about Jesus. What an adventure! And what a challenge! It's exciting to think about what God might have in store for you—maybe getting baptised or seeing friends get baptised. Maybe seeing healings and miracles, doing mission work in a faraway place, pushing back darkness, hosting a church in your home, community transformation... Life following Jesus isn't easy, but it is exciting!

Read It: Acts 16 v 14, 25-26, 29-31

> *One of those listening was a woman from the city of Thyatira named Lydia, a dealer in purple cloth. She was a worshipper of God. The Lord opened her heart to respond to Paul's message.*
>
> *[Some time later, in prison...]*
>
> *About midnight Paul and Silas were praying and singing hymns to God, and the other prisoners were listening to them. Suddenly there was such a violent earthquake that the foundations of the prison were shaken. At once all the prison doors flew open, and everyone's chains came loose ...*
>
> *The jailer called for lights, rushed in and fell trembling before Paul and Silas. He then brought them out and asked, "Sirs, what must I do to be saved?"*
>
> *They replied, "Believe in the Lord Jesus, and you will be saved—you and your household."*

Discuss It

- *Who were the first people to respond to the message about Jesus in Philippi?*
- *Would they be the people you would pick to start a church? Explain.*
- *What does this story show us about who the church is for?*
- *How does it make you feel to think about the adventures God has lined up for you?*

Pray It

Dear God, thank you for how you worked through Paul to tell people about Jesus and start new churches. Help me to join in with other Christians who are serious about telling people about you and let me see you work powerfully through my life. Get me ready for the adventures you have lined up for me. Amen.

Do It

Draw a picture of, or write down, a couple of ideas about how God could use you now and in the future.

DAY 44

New Creation: Home Time!

REVELATION 21 – 22

Our Story

Imagine that you could create the perfect place. What would it smell, sound and look like? What would you do there? What would not be allowed in? What would you no longer need if it was perfect?

God's Story

Life for Christians was far from perfect in AD 90, 60 years after Jesus returned to heaven. Paul and almost all of Jesus' first disciples are dead, killed by people who don't like the church. Jesus' friend John is an old man, imprisoned on the Greek island of Patmos for his faith. In today's story God reveals to John how he is working behind the scenes and shows him our future heavenly home. There are lots of layers of hidden meaning in what John sees. Still, when an angel commands him to record everything he's shown, he does. It's all in the book we call Revelation.

New Creation Story

What John glimpsed blew his mind, knocked his socks off, and filled his heart to bursting. It made him more courageous and more determined to endure hardship for Jesus: what perfection, harmony, beauty, joy, peace, holiness and hope! Words weren't enough, comparisons were limited, but he'd try to record what the angel had revealed to him...

In the new heaven and earth that John had been shown, several things were, well, different. There was no sun or moon because God shone so brightly. The gates never shut because the heavenly city was safe. There was no death, sin, crying, pain, brokenness, loneliness or exhaustion. There was no Satan-snake. There was nothing bad. Everything was good. Everything was new. Everything was perfect.

And at the centre of everything was the best thing of all: Jesus. John meditated on the revelations of Jesus he'd had: white as snow, wearing a gold sash, eyes like blazing fire, voice like rushing waters, face like the sun, shining in all its brilliance. Tattooed on Jesus' thigh he'd seen the words, "King of kings and Lord of lords". He sat as a Lamb and King, centre stage, on an awesome ruby red and diamond-like throne, a rainbow aura surrounding him. Lightning and peals of thunder accompanied thousands of angels and creatures and people from all nations chanting "Holy!" and "Worthy!" and "Hallelujah!" Their songs told the truth of how he created everything and kept it all going and how all power and majesty and salvation were his.

In the visions a huge new city of Jerusalem had come down from heaven. It was pure gold, brilliant and bright from God's glory. It dazzled with jewels and precious stones. The thick, tall walls were made from a gemstone called jasper. And twelve pearl gates were guarded by twelve angels.

A crystal-clear river of living water flowed from the throne where Jesus sat. Besides this river two trees of life grew, trees just like the tree of life in Eden, growing fruit that could be picked every month. Their leaves brought healing to the nations.

This new heaven and new earth felt like home. Jesus was reigning and ruling at the centre of it all. He was magnetic. "Who would not want to be here with Jesus for ever?" John thought. Why would anyone resist the ongoing invitation to be a part of all this, even when it was really hard to live for Jesus? This was what lay ahead for John, and for all of God's forgiven people—being with Jesus, part of his forever family, in this perfect place.

God's Story

John's incredible visions were sent to persecuted churches to remind them that Jesus was still King of heaven and was still in control, and that God would keep all his promises in the end, so that one day pain, death and evil would be a thing of the past. The future new heaven and earth that John saw in his vision will be even better than the Garden of Eden, because they will never end and evil will never take root there. This life is only a dress rehearsal for a greater life to come. This is the happiest of happily-ever-afters.

Our Story

We have learned a lot in our journey through the greatest story ever. As we finish, take a moment to consider—are you a friend of Jesus and have you received his wonderful gift of eternal life? When we make this most important decision of all, God's story becomes *our* story—for ever.

Read It: Revelation 22 v 1-4, 17

> *Then the angel showed me the river of the water of life, as clear as crystal, flowing from the throne of God and of the Lamb down the middle of the great street of the city. On each side of the river stood the tree of life, bearing twelve crops of fruit, yielding its fruit every month. And the leaves of the tree are for the healing of the nations. No longer will there be any curse. The throne of God and of the Lamb will be in the city, and his servants will serve him. They will see his face, and his name will be on their foreheads … Let the one who is thirsty come; and let the one who wishes take the free gift of the water of life.*

Discuss It

- *People have strange ideas about what eternity will be like. Which of the following does John actually see in the part of the vision he was given of heaven that we just read? A golden city / Trees with fruit / People playing harps / Cherubs floating on clouds / Ghosts spooking people / A river of life / A throne and a king / A lamb*
- *Who gets to live in this perfect forever place? Have you responded to King Jesus' invitation to come and be in friendship with him?*
- *What are you most looking forward to in this new creation and why?*
- *What have you most enjoyed about our journey through the greatest story ever told?*

Pray It

Dear God, thank you for the promise of a perfect new creation. Thank you that if we are following Jesus as our King and Saviour and friend, one day we will be there with you. Help us not to fear death or worry too much about this life, but to keep eternity in sight. Help us to live for the things that really matter. Amen.

Do It

Amazing. You've finished. Well done!

Now have a go at telling the greatest story ever, from start to finish, in two minutes. Make sure you include:

- Eden
- Abraham
- Passover
- David
- Malachi
- Jesus (obviously!)
- The new heavens and new earth.

You will need to talk fast!

Celebratory Optional Do It

(Ask an adult about the best time to do this. They may prefer that you do it after school or at another time in the week.)

In Revelation, the last book in the Bible, John sees the name "Jesus" on the foreheads of people in heaven who have followed him. Grab a pen, find a forehead and write "Jesus" on it—but check first if they have decided to follow him and be his friend.

DAY 45

Memory Verse

"You will receive power when the Holy Spirit comes upon you; and you will be my witnesses."

ACTS 1 v 8

VERSE-MEMORISING TOP TIPS

Write It
Visualise It
Act It
Sing It
Record It
Use an App
... and repeat, repeat, repeat!

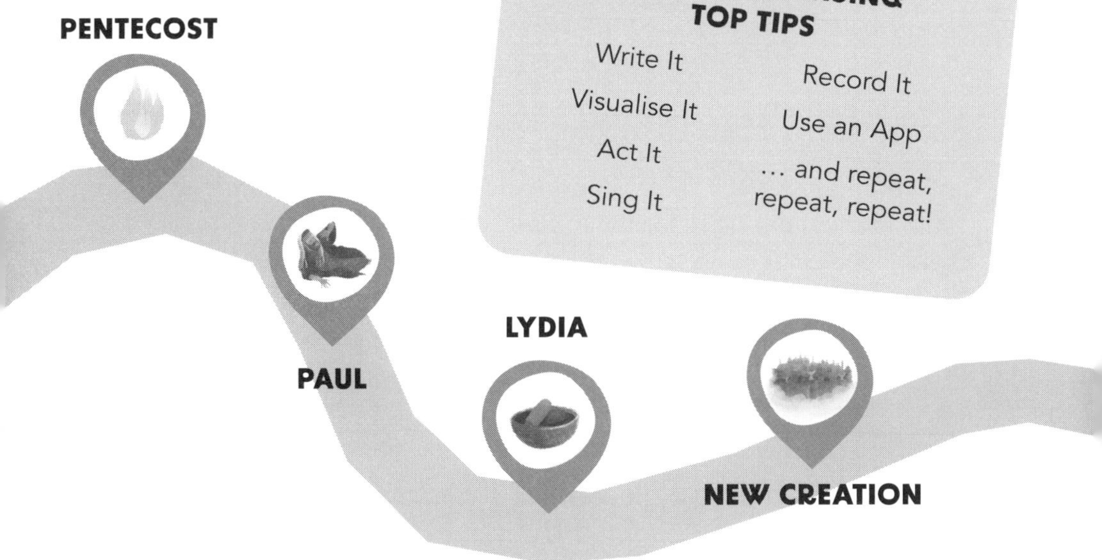